The Elem

Joseph Sheppherd fifteen. He was born in the United States in 1949 into a family of Californian cattlemen and fruit farmers. His membership of the Bahá'í Faith at an early age sparked his interest in the diversity of culture and language in the world. As an anthropologist he has travelled extensively through more than fifty countries and carried out research in Guatemala, Colombia, Cameroon and Equatorial Guinea, where he worked for two years as the Anthropological Advisor to the Government, and Curator of National Ethnological and Archaeological Museum in Malabo. He received his Bachelor's Degree with Honours in Anthropology from the University of California, and his Master's Degree in Archaeology from the University of Cambridge. He presently lectures at the American College in London and writes from his home in Oxford, where he is finishing his Doctorate.

Joseph Sheppherd is the author of: *Mama Buzurg is Coming, Guebe and the Toy Truck,* and *A Leaf of Honey and the Proverbs of the Rainforest.*

The *Elements Of* is a series designed to present high quality introductions to a broad range of essential subjects.

The books are commissioned specifically from experts in their fields. They provide readable and often unique views of the various topics covered, and are therefore of interest both to those who have some knowledge of the subject, as well as those who are approaching it for the first time.

Many of these concise yet comprehensive books have practical suggestions and exercises which allow personal experience as well as theoretical understanding, and offer a valuable source of information on many important themes.

In the same series

> **the elements of**

the bahá'í faith

joseph sheppherd

ELEMENT

Shaftesbury, Dorset • Rockport • Massachusetts • Melbourne, Australia

© Element Books Limited, 1992
Text © Joseph Sheppherd 1992

First published in Great Britain in 1992 by
Element Books Limited
Shaftesbury, Dorset SP7 8BP

Published in the USA in 1992 by
Element Books, Inc.
PO Box 830, Rockport, MA 01966

Published in Australia in 1992 by
Element Books and
distributed by Penguin Books Australia Limited
487 Maroondah Highway, Ringwood,
Victoria 3134

Reprinted 1993

Reissued 1997

All rights reserved.
No part of this book may be reproduced or utilized
in any form or by any means, electronical or mechanical,
without prior permission in writing from the Publisher.

Cover design by Max Fairbrother
Typeset by Falcon Typographic Art Ltd, Fife, Scotland
Printed and bound in Great Britain by
Biddles Ltd, Guildford and King's Lynn

British Library Cataloguing in Publication
data available

Library of Congress Cataloging in Publication
data available

ISBN 1–86204–145–8

This book is dedicated
to my mother
Greta
with much love
and to the memory of
Lucile Jordan
of Bell Mountain

It is not for him to pride himself who loveth his own country, but rather for him who loveth the whole world. The earth is but one country, and mankind its citizens. GWB:CXVII

Bahá'u'lláh

CONTENTS

PREFACE

Although this survey of the Bahá'í Faith endeavours to present a clear and succinct introduction to the origins, basic teachings and way of life of the religion, it is offered with the humble knowledge that it is far from complete in its description of the life and mission of Bahá'u'lláh, the Founder of the Bahá'í Faith. I have tried to write especially for the reader who may know nothing more than the name 'Bahá'í' and who is interested to find out a little about the religion. At the same time, I have attempted to construct my explanations in such a way that those who perhaps have a Bahá'í friend or relative and therefore know something of the religion, but who lack an overall picture, may gain a more coherent understanding of the subject. Many learned scholars have written biographies of the life of Bahá'u'lláh and I could have quoted from these. I have, however, declined to do this because I wanted to tell the story of Bahá'u'lláh as it was told to me, and to explain as simply as possible His teachings.

Bahá'u'lláh wrote in two languages, Persian and Arabic, and of the hundred or so volumes He wrote during His lifetime, a substantial number have been translated into English. Because this year marks the 100th anniversary of His passing, it seemed appropriate to draw passages from some of these translations and include them in the text.

No book is ever written alone, and I would like to acknowledge the assistance of my friends Johanna O'Connor, Tak Sum Ho, Thelma Batchelor and Andy Scott. I am also grateful to Phillip Hall-Patch, Gandhimohan Viswanathan, Richard Goodson, and Tiffani Betts of the Oxford University Bahá'í Society for reading the text and offering suggestions.

Oxford, England
16 February 1992 AD
10 Mulk 148 BE

PART 1
INTRODUCTION

1·WHO ARE THE BAHÁ'ÍS?

About thirty years ago, a friend by the name of Lucile Jordan lent a couple of books to my mother and me. At the time it was not possible to see how this simple act would change the course of my life, but looking back this was the event which led me to discover the Bahá'í Faith. Now, three decades later, I know that many Bahá'ís would tell how their first introduction to the Faith came through the loan of a book.

Lucile was a kind-hearted old lady who was employed by the same hospital where my mother worked as a nurse. Even though she lived some distance from us in the sparsely populated area around Bell Mountain, we visited each other regularly. Distances between neighbours and friends are greater in the Mojave Desert than other places in California. Even in the arid and optimistically named Apple Valley where we lived, there were few houses nearby. Bell Mountain was even worse; it was more a community of tumbleweeds and sagebrush than people. Knowing that my mother and I were interested in religion, Lucile lent us the books.

Like many people living in the desert, we were interested in God but not very impressed with churches. Over the years we had attended, on one occasion or another, every church in the surrounding towns to hear what they had to say, but we were not members of any particular faith. They all seemed to be vying with one another for the exclusive rights on God, each one insisting that their church was the only true religion. Competition was fierce to attract membership among the scant inhabitants of the desert, and preachers went to extreme lengths. For example, in desperation one preacher erected a small white picket fence around a well-watered square metre of grass in front of his church. He informed his congregation that when Jesus returned to earth, this tiny grassy square was the precise spot where His foot would first touch the ground as He descended from heaven. I think it was at this point we stopped going there!

The best information about God and religion was to be found not in the pulpit but in books; and so with no further churches to attend in the area, we contented ourselves with reading. Books were a part of our household and lifestyle, and my mother taught me that books were not mere decorations or units of good intentions. Bookshelves were designed to hold books you had already read and wished to read again. As I grew up, I inherited my mother's voracious appetite for knowledge, and her belief that people are what they read. From looking at our bookshelves anyone could tell that we were seekers.

Knowing this, Lucile lent us some books about a religion we had never heard of: the Bahá'í Faith. In the evening of the day she received them, my mother sat down in a chair and began to read, and when I went to bed she was still reading. In the morning when I woke up, she was still awake, sitting there with a book in her hands. By now the table beside her was covered with other books laid open and stacked on top of each other. My mother had not only read both of Lucile's books in one night, she had been comparing what they said with other books we had in the house.

That morning when she got to work, she asked Lucile if she were a member of this religion, if she were a *Bahá'í*. The word was new and she did not know exactly how to pronounce it, or for that matter what it meant. She discovered that Lucile did not know either. Lucile was not a Bahá'í – the books had been given to her by someone else whose name and phone number were written inside the cover. She had not had a chance to read them before my mother borrowed them.

That evening my mother phoned the number. I remember how the conversation began. My mother introduced herself and said: 'I have a houseful of books on religion. How is it I have never heard of the Bahá'í Faith before?' My mother could be very direct, and I could only imagine the other side of the conversation. She continued: 'You people must be the best kept secret in the universe. I've been looking for you for twenty years. I knew that there must be a religion like this out there somewhere, I just didn't know what it was called.'

After a lifetime of searching for the truth it had, in a sense, found her. It was amazing that it had taken so long to discover the Bahá'í Faith, because once we knew what it was, it was easy to find. There were Bahá'ís everywhere – we kept running into them. There were books about the Bahá'í Faith in the public library, and entries in the dictionary and encyclopedia. It was even listed in the phone book. It had been there all along; we just hadn't seen it.

My mother went through a remarkable transformation. Within a few weeks she had gone to visit the lady she had spoken to on the telephone, read half a dozen other books on the religion, and become a Bahá'í. Soon afterwards, when Lucile was able to get the books back and read them for herself, she decided that she was a Bahá'í also.

I had to wait my turn to read the books. In the meantime my mother explained what she had found in her reading, and for days we talked about nothing else. The Bahá'í Faith was a real discovery. I found the story fascinating: I learned that a new Messenger of God had lived in the middle of the last century in a place called Persia. His name was *Bahá'u'lláh* which translated into English meant 'Glory of God'; and the people who followed His teachings were *Bahá'ís*, literally 'followers of Bahá'u'lláh'.

Bahá'u'lláh had brought a new set of teachings which held the answers to the modern world's problems. Eventually, when I could get hold of some books and read them for myself, I found Bahá'u'lláh's explanations were extraordinarily profound and insightful concerning the spiritual and social needs of humanity. My favourite book of His was entitled *Hidden Words*. It was a compilation of moral aphorisms full of ethical wisdom – a distillation of the spiritual guidance of all the Revelations of the past. I read and re-read the passages. Now things seemed to make sense.

When I started using in school what I was learning at home, my teachers must have thought that I had had a brain transplant. I remember the stunned expression on one English teacher's face when she asked me to use the word 'justice' in a sentence. 'Beyond a sort of vague ideal,' I replied, 'it is difficult to know what justice looks like in an age so burdened with tyranny. Justice can only be possible among people who are free from the prejudices of race, nationality and gender. In a way, injustice blinds us to the reality of justice. In its absence, we are forced to guess what it looks like. I feel people are mistaken to think of it as some kind of product. Justice itself is not an end, it is the means to greater things, it is the means to seeing and understanding things for ourselves.'

The teacher was not used to hearing such answers from the mouth of such a bored, lacklustre and apparently clueless student. In the silence which ensued in the wake of my answer, I forgot to tell them that the reason I had these thoughts was because I had been reading books by Bahá'u'lláh. Fortunately, the class bell rang about then!

School was never the same after that, and teachers were no longer boring. I was interested in their ideas. In fact, the entire educational process now had meaning, and I was beginning to understand that education was not exclusively found in schools. Ultimately, teachers do not teach students, they get students to teach themselves. I was twelve years old at the time. I suddenly realized one day, in the middle of my science class, that my education was my own responsibility and there were no limits in the world except the ones I imposed upon myself through neglect of my studies. This also applied to my spiritual education. This realization led to many others about myself and the lifetime that lay ahead; being twelve became an age of wonder and discovery.

At that time, I did not know what I wanted to be, what

profession or career to follow. One day I wanted to be an artist, the next a scientist, and the day after something else. This diversity of interest did not really concern me – it was normal for twelve-year-olds to vacillate between future professions from one minute to the next. (Even at forty-two, I still sometimes wonder what I want to be when I grow up.)

However, back then I did worry about being inconsistent with my religious interests, for I had begun to take religion seriously. I realized that religions are not like professions; people should not change them just because they want a change. I knew that I believed in the teachings of Bahá'u'lláh, and I knew that I wanted to be a Bahá'í more than anything else. But I was young and I wondered if I would change my mind later. I decided to wait and look at other religions again before I became a Bahá'í. If, after more investigation and comparison, I still believed in Bahá'u'lláh, I would know that I could become a sincere Bahá'í.

Looking back, I can now see that this was a mature decision. But at the time I think it was influenced by something my mother pointed out to me. She informed me that in the Bahá'í Faith children were not automatically born into the religion or expected to follow blindly the religious choices of their parents. Children decided for themselves if and when they wanted to become Bahá'ís. This meant that even though my mother had become a Bahá'í, I could still choose my own religion. I considered this and decided to wait until I was older before I registered as a Bahá'í, so that I would be sure that I was adopting a religion because I believed in it myself, independently of my mother. I had read in the writings of Bahá'u'lláh that the age of maturity began at fifteen. I chose to wait until then to make my decision.

2·WHERE DO BAHÁ'ÍS WORSHIP AND MEET?

By the time I was fifteen, my mother and I had moved to Germany and were living in a little village named Sembach near the city of Kaiserslautern. The shady strolls along the leaf-strewn paths through dark forests and grassy meadows were quite a contrast to the sandstorm-swept treks we had previously made across expanses of desert randomly dotted by the occasional cactus and Joshua tree.

In the past three years, we had not only travelled to Europe, but to many places within the United States meeting Bahá'ís from other cultures. The Navajo Bahá'ís invited Indians and non-Indians alike from all over America to join them in a week-long conference and cultural festival. My mother and I went. Looking back, I think that it was that week of listening to the ancient legends of the Indians who attended the festival that sparked my interest in anthropology.

Two weeks after my fifteenth birthday, Bahá'ís from around the world began to arrive in a small town called Langenhain on a hill overlooking Frankfurt, just a few hours' drive from our home in Sembach near the French border. Langenhain had been chosen some years before as the site of the first Bahá'í House of Worship in Europe. An elegantly beautiful nine-sided temple had been constructed symbolizing the unity of all the world's religions. It was to be dedicated on the 4th of July 1964, and I chose that day to declare my faith in Bahá'u'lláh and register as a Bahá'í.

When my mother and I arrived, there were already more than a thousand people present. I had never seen such a diverse gathering. Every continent and scores of countries were represented by Bahá'ís from every race and of every colour. They greeted each other as friends and associated without reticence or prejudice. It was then that I began to understand Bahá'u'lláh's teaching of 'unity in diversity'. It is one thing to read about a principle which says that unity in the world is only achievable if the individual races and cultures are appreciated, but quite another to see it in practice. The dedication ceremony was uplifting and simple. Bahá'í prayers were read in German, Persian, English, Swedish, French and Spanish; as were passages from the holy scriptures of various religions – the Old and New Testaments, the Bhagavad Gita, and the Qur'án.

In the afternoon, when the dedication ceremony was complete, and people began their journeys home, I found a quiet spot beside the House of Worship and wrote a note to the Bahá'í Centre in Frankfurt-on-Main that I wished to be registered as a member. Since that day twenty-eight years ago, I have been a Bahá'í. As a story about finding the truth and embracing a new religion, this is perhaps less dramatic than many I have heard. However, the process of personal transformation which resulted from studying the teachings of Bahá'u'lláh was just as profound for me as for those whose lives were salvaged from destruction by becoming Bahá'ís.

Soon after the dedication of the Bahá'í House of Worship, my mother and I moved back to California. In the three years in which we had been away, the Bahá'í Faith had grown substantially. Many people were doing what my mother and I had done: investigating the Bahá'í Faith.

By now, there were many more people of my own age who had somehow met a Bahá'í or had read a book by Bahá'u'lláh and had become Bahá'ís themselves. Because we were young, we automatically gravitated together. In the midst of the hedonism of the hippy movement and

Bahá'í House of Worship, Langenhain, Germany

the demonstrations against the war in Vietnam, our group of Bahá'í youth were doing what we could to solve some of the social ills of the times by telling others about what we had learned from the teachings of Bahá'u'lláh. Some people listened. Every weekend we hosted meetings to which we invited our classmates and friends to discuss how to overcome the obstacles which stood in the way of achieving peace and unity in the world. Some towns had Bahá'í Centres where we could meet but, where the Bahá'í community was still small in numbers, we met in each other's homes.

It is much the same today, although there are many more Bahá'í Centres and many more Bahá'í homes where people gather, pray, read from the writings of Bahá'u'lláh, discuss the issues at hand, and enjoy the fellowship of each other. The place where Bahá'ís meet is not important. Bahá'u'lláh reminds us that:

> Blessed is the spot, and the house, and the place, and the city, and the heart, and the mountain, and the refuge, and the cave, and the valley, and the land, and the sea, and the island, and meadow where mention of God has been made, and His praise glorified. BP:iii

I have good memories of those times. The friends I made when I was young are now grown up and scattered all over the globe. It is the same for me as I now live in Oxford, in England. Except for Bahá'í conferences, I rarely see them now. Just as I have decided to be an anthropologist, so they have all chosen professions in which they can find ways to use their talents to serve mankind. They are farmers, ecologists, teachers, biologists, physicists, social workers, doctors, journalists, and above all, parents. They are bringing up their children to love mankind, and by example teaching them to treat each other with equality and justice. They are putting into practice the Bahá'í way of life.

Now, wherever my anthropological work takes me in the world, I meet a new generation of Bahá'ís who are carrying on the responsibility of promoting an ever-advancing

Bahá'í House of Worship, Wilmette, Illinois, USA

civilization. Whenever I am close enough I try to visit a Bahá'í House of Worship. There are now many more in the world. To date there are seven, one for each continent. They are located in: Wilmette, Illinois, USA; Kampala, Uganda; Langenhain near Frankfurt, Germany; Sydney, Australia; Apia, Western Samoa; Panama City, Panama; and New Delhi, India.

Lucile Jordan passed away a few years ago, a Bahá'í who truly loved Bahá'u'lláh and who served humanity in her day-to-day work among the poor and needy. I am very grateful for the rôle she and my mother played in my becoming a Bahá'í. Although Lucile was not a relative, she was a kind of spiritual ancestor in a continuum of people who discovered the teachings of Bahá'u'lláh and passed the knowledge on to others like me. After all these years, it is ironic to be asked to write a book about the Bahá'í Faith, which may itself be lent to others like the books she lent to me.

PART 2
BAHÁ'U'LLÁH

3·THE ORIGINS OF THE BAHÁ'Í FAITH

At the origin and centre of any religion is the Founder; He, not His followers, is the One who defines the religion. The Messenger of God, not the interpretations or limited ideas of those who come after, is the standard by which we should evaluate a religion. In every respect, Bahá'u'lláh is the foundation of the Bahá'í Faith, and the pivot around which revolve all the teachings and principles of His religion. To know Bahá'u'lláh is to read His writings; therein lies the essence of the Messenger of God.

I find my words to be inadequate in describing Him; no description or characterization seems to be satisfactory. How can I describe Bahá'u'lláh's majesty, His essential holiness and radiance of being, in a way in which you can share the esteem and reverence I feel when I read passages of His writings? Only reading them for yourself will achieve this. Even the contemporary historians who witnessed and recorded the unparalleled events of His life were often left wordless in their attempt to describe Bahá'u'lláh Himself.

The best attempt occurred just two years before His death when Bahá'u'lláh received one of the few Westerners ever to meet Him. The visitor was Edward Granville Browne, a rising young orientalist and future professor from Cambridge

University in England. Years later, describing his meeting with Bahá'u'lláh, Browne wrote:

> Though I dimly suspected whither I was going and whom I was to behold (for no distinct intimation had been given me), a second or two elapsed ere, with a throb of wonder and awe, I became definitely conscious that the room was not untenanted. In the corner where the divan met the wall sat a wondrous and venerable figure . . . The face of Him on whom I gazed I can never forget, though I cannot describe it. Those piercing eyes seemed to read one's very soul; power and authority sat on that ample brow . . . No need to ask in whose presence I stood, as I bowed myself before one who is the object of a devotion and love which kings might envy and emperors sigh for in vain! A mild dignified voice bade me be seated.

Bahá'u'lláh spoke these words to Browne:

> Praise be to God that thou hast attained! . . . Thou hast come to see a prisoner and exile . . . We desire but the good of the world and the happiness of the nations; yet they deem Us a stirrer up of strife and sedition worthy of bondage and banishment . . . That all nations should become one in faith and all men as brothers; that the bonds of affection and unity between the sons of men should be strengthened; that diversity of religion should cease, and the differences of race be annulled – what harm is there in this? . . . Yet so shall it be; these fruitless strifes, these ruinous wars shall pass away, and the 'Most Great Peace' shall come . . . Yet do We see your kings and rulers lavishing their treasures more freely on means of destruction of the human race than on that which would conduce to the happiness of mankind . . . These strifes and this bloodshed and discord must cease, and all men be as one kindred and one family . . . Let not a man glory in this, that he loves his country; let him rather glory in this, that he loves his kind . . . PB:v

There are no satisfactory words to portray the character or personality of Bahá'u'lláh, or for that matter the nature of Messengerhood itself. In the past, people have tried to describe in retrospect Moses, Jesus, or Muhammad, but have failed to capture the spirit of adoration with which the earliest apostles and disciples held the Messenger of God. Over the years, little by little, people finally settled on a handful of designations for the Messenger of God for their age: words like Prophet, Seer, Revelator, Mouthpiece, Saviour, Messiah, Redeemer, Enlightened One. These are our impoverished efforts to describe something which has come from God and is beyond our vocabulary.

It is the same for Bahá'u'lláh. In a sense, describing the Messenger of God is like describing the sun. I can describe the sun's light and warmth, but in the end words fail to convey its reality. Perhaps the best portrayal of both the sun and the Messenger of God requires the analogy of the mirror: like a perfect mirror placed in the sunlight, Bahá'u'lláh, in common with all the past Messengers, reflects the Glory of God. Bahá'u'lláh and these Messengers are not God, just as the reflection in the mirror is not the sun. Although the bright reflection and the sun itself appear equal, both shedding their light and warmth upon us, they are separate. It is impossible for us to approach the sun without being consumed in a mighty force beyond our comprehension, but we can draw near to the reflection in the mirror and understand something of the light and power of the sun. In the same sense, the Messenger is the intermediary between God and man, the mirror in whose reflection we can see the attributes of God.

The concept of an intermediary is expressed in one of the symbols of the Bahá'í Faith. Bahá'ís wishing to wear a symbol of their religion sometimes use this as an emblem on a ring. The symbol has two basic elements: the design itself and the calligraphic Arabic letters it contains. Firstly, as a design, the horizonal strokes represent, from top to bottom, the world of God, the Creator; the world of the Messenger and His Cause; and the world of man, the creation. The vertical line is a repeat of the middle horizontal line: the world of

A symbol of the Bahá'í faith

the Messenger, thus joining the world of the Creator with that of His creation. The two five-pointed stars to either side of the middle line represent the human body, as well as symbolizing the two Messengers for this age – Bahá'u'lláh and His forerunner, the Báb. The design is composed of the Arabic letters 'b' and 'h' which stand for the consonants in the words Bahá and Báb, the titles of the two most recent Messengers of God. Often, in classical Arabic the vowels are not written or included in calligraphy.

During the first years of being a Bahá'í, I wondered what Bahá'u'lláh looked like and what it would have been like to travel to visit Him in prison as so many early Bahá'ís did during His lifetime. I am sure these kinds of thoughts are common not just to Bahá'ís but to anyone who loves the Founder of their Faith. People cannot help but wonder what it was like to live during the times of the Messenger of God, to have been able to meet Moses or Jesus or Muhammad.

As a child, I grew up seeing paintings of Jesus on the walls of churches and in the homes of my schoolmates. Jesus lived long before the invention of the camera and photography, so these were of course artists' conceptions. Looking at them, I always wondered if Jesus was being portrayed in the race of the artist. He was usually painted in the centre foreground as a tall, blue-eyed, blond-haired man against a background of darker people. Jesus appeared as if He were a

Scandinavian or northern European like my ancestors. This was unrealistic. Jesus was born into a Jewish family in a remote eastern outpost of the Roman Empire. In Palestine, in that part of the Levant where He was born, the people were and are racially dark, both in the colour of their eyes and hair. Later I discovered that artists from different races and countries tended to produce portraits of a Jesus with which they could identify. White artists painted Jesus white, black artists painted Him black. I began to understand how misleading these portraits were. In many ways, they made racism religiously justifiable in the minds of some people.

It would be better to have no imaginary portraits of Jesus at all, either on the walls of rooms or within the minds of people. It would be better to replace these exterior and interior pictures with the words and actions of Jesus. It would be better to concentrate on His teachings than to attach false significance to the imagination of an artist.

Nevertheless, I wondered what Bahá'u'lláh looked like. He lived during a time in which photography had been invented, and I discovered that one photograph did exist, but I would have to visit the Holy Land to see it. Copies were not made and I would have to wait until I could go on pilgrimage to the Bahá'í World Centre. Having been born in 1949, a photograph was the nearest I could get to meeting Bahá'u'lláh Himself.

By the time I was born, I had missed living during Bahá'u'lláh's lifetime by fifty-seven years. As a very young Bahá'í, part of me regretted having been born too late. But then I began to realize that even if I had been born a hundred years sooner, there would have been no guarantee that I would have known about Bahá'u'lláh, much less have met Him. Only a few of the people alive during His lifetime heard about Bahá'u'lláh, and only a few of those recognized him as a Messenger of God. In my native country of the United States, the first mention of the Bahá'í Faith was not until 1892 at a presentation at the World's Columbian Exposition in Chicago. This was the same year in which Bahá'u'lláh died. It was two years before the first American, Thornton Chase, became a Bahá'í.

It takes time for the news of the existence of the Messenger of God to spread. It was the same during the lifetime of Jesus – few people outside Judaea, Galilee and Samaria were aware of His existence, and relatively few people within those three regions actually arose to follow Him. Christianity took centuries to reach America – depending on whether you read Irish, Viking or Spanish history, it was either 554, 1,121, or 1,497 years before the first Christian reached the shores of North America. And it was not until 1,500 years after the death of Jesus that the first anonymous native American became a Christian.

Reading biographies about Bahá'u'lláh's life answered many questions about what it was like to be alive during His lifetime, but in 1967 I had the privilege of meeting someone who had actually met Bahá'u'lláh personally. This was living history.

His name was Tarázu'lláh Samandarí and at that time he was probably one of the last people alive to have been in the presence of Bahá'u'lláh. Mr Samandarí's father had been one of the nineteen Apostles of Bahá'u'lláh, and as a young man his son had journeyed overland from his native Persia to 'Akká to meet Him. When I heard that Mr Samandarí was staying for a few days in Los Angeles, I hitch-hiked down from Apple Valley to meet him. I was not surprised to find the room full of fellow Bahá'ís when I arrived. It seemed that many of us had had the same idea. We had all recognized that this was an opportunity which would not come again. Tarázu'lláh Samandarí was a very old man of ninety-two, and his son Mihdí, who was himself quite old, translated for his father.

I sat on the floor in the crowded living-room and listened as Mr Samandarí told the story of the occasions on which he had been in the presence of Bahá'u'lláh. He was seventeen when he first made the long trip from Persia to the Turkish penal colony of 'Akká where Bahá'u'lláh had been incarcerated for more than twenty years. The trip had taken many weeks, but had been worth it. For a period of six months he had been in the company of Bahá'u'lláh's family, and on several occasions had heard

Him reveal the words of God as He dictated tablets and prayers.

Every scene was there like a photograph in his mind. As he described the events that he had witnessed, even the smallest detail was included. He told how on one occasion he was asked by Bahá'u'lláh to distribute roses to all the people present; he cherished the honour of having provided even this small and simple service. His stories were like small windows on a different time and place which we could see through his eyes. He had seen the early Bahá'ís coming on foot as pilgrims from far away in an effort to witness for themselves the author of the teachings they had read and adopted as their religion. During the first years of Bahá'u'lláh's imprisonment, pilgrims would arrive at the prison gate and beg to be admitted. This would leave the prison guards bewildered. They could not understand why anyone would want to try to get *into* prison.

Those who were allowed to enter would stay for weeks or months in the foulest and most squalid of conditions just to be near the Messenger of God. Disease at that time was rampant in the prison city, and the pilgrims ran the very real risk of contracting something fatal, and dying before they could leave. Sometimes the pilgrims were turned away and not allowed entrance. They would have to content themselves with standing on the far side of the double moat which surrounded the city, and seeing only Bahá'u'lláh's hand as He waved to them through the barred window of His cell. Broken-hearted, they would return on foot the hundreds of miles back to their homelands having seen only His hand.

As Mr Samandarí described what he had seen, we sat enwrapped in the images of his words. He had been fortunate to arrive during a time in which people were more freely allowed to visit Bahá'u'lláh. The personality of Bahá'u'lláh finally won over the guards and the governor of the prison city himself. They recognized His guiltlessness, and without the authority of their governmental superiors, permitted Him to live outside the walls of 'Akká.

Via his translator, Mr Samandarí humbly described Bahá'u'lláh's majesty and kindness; the memories of a time when he was a youth of my age of seventeen. When he was finished, some of us asked questions about what it was like to have been a Bahá'í during the time of the Messenger of God Himself. He told of the honour he had in serving Bahá'u'lláh both during His life and afterwards, and that it is the duty of everyone to respond to the needs of the times in which they live and to do what they can as Bahá'ís.

I realized then that in a sense I had not missed meeting Bahá'u'lláh. I had not missed knowing about Him – I had read His books and recognized the divine origin of His teachings. I had even met someone who had met Him. Above all, I had become a Bahá'í. It was not important that I had not seen Bahá'u'lláh with my own eyes or heard the tones of His voice with my own ears; His words and teachings were what mattered. The Message was still here even if the Messenger of God had gone away.

Someone in the room then asked about the passing of Bahá'u'lláh. Mr Samandarí's voice was suddenly sorrowful as he reluctantly recounted how he had been amongst the visiting pilgrims and resident Bahá'ís from around 'Akká who were summoned to the presence of Bahá'u'lláh while He was lying ill in bed, being tended by His family. As he stood there as a young man so many years ago, Mr Samandarí realized that Bahá'u'lláh was dying.

He paused for a while and then repeated what Bahá'u'lláh had told the grief-stricken assembly of devoted Bahá'ís. His voice was clear, but softer because of the fever He had contracted. He spoke about the importance of unity. From the way Mr Samandarí spoke and his humble gestures, even before the words were translated from Persian, it was obvious with what love he regarded Bahá'u'lláh. Before excusing himself and retiring for the night, Mr Samandarí gave us the same message Bahá'u'lláh had given him: that we should be united and seek to promote unity in the world.

In 1978, as a pilgrim myself, I travelled to Israel, and the former prison city of 'Akká, and visited nearby Bahjí, the resting place of Bahá'u'lláh. For the Bahá'ís, Bahjí is the holiest place on earth, the Qiblih of the Bahá'í Faith; the place towards which Bahá'ís turn in prayer. The simple

Entrance to the Shrine of Bahá'u'lláh

and dignified shrine which encloses His tomb beneath it, is adjacent to where young Samandarí had met Bahá'u'lláh and where He had passed away. After I had bowed and humbly placed my forehead at the threshold of the room over Bahá'u'lláh's tomb, I prayed for the enlightenment of my own soul and for the peace and unity of the nations of the earth.

Later that day, I crossed the Bay of 'Akká to the slopes of Mount Carmel, the mountain spoken of by Isaiah as the 'mountain of the Lord'. Part of every pilgrimage is a visit to the Shrine of the Báb, the resting place of the Herald-Prophet who announced the coming of Bahá'u'lláh. Set among the gardens, monuments and buildings of the Bahá'í World Centre above Haifa on Mount Carmel is the International Bahá'í Archives in which the only photograph of Bahá'u'lláh is kept. Every Bahá'í pilgrim has an opportunity to view it, and as I stood before it I finally knew what Bahá'u'lláh looked like. Like Professor Browne, I cannot describe the face I saw in that small photograph.

The picture showed Bahá'u'lláh seated in a chair with one arm resting on a table. He was wearing an abba which flowed from His shoulders down to the ground. He was bearded, and His head was covered with a turban, the kind worn by people from this part of the world in the latter half of the nineteenth century. I knew the historical circumstances of the photograph. Bahá'u'lláh was being exiled yet again and this was an official photograph of a prisoner. There was seriousness and profound resolve in His tired yet radiant face. This was the countenance of the Messenger of God, the Lord of the Age Who had borne the torture, imprisonment and banishment of His enemies from the birth of His religion. Looking at the photograph, I suddenly realized that it really did not matter whether or not I knew what Bahá'u'lláh looked like. The love I felt for him transcended any mental image. It was His teachings which were important.

As I stood there with the other pilgrims, I remembered what I had read of the life of the man in the photograph. It was a story which began many years before His exiles and imprisonment. The actual birth of the Bahá'í Faith

The Shrine of the Báb

began in the city of Shíráz, Persia, on the night of the 22nd of May 1844. The middle of the nineteenth century was a time of great messianic expectation in the world. Throughout Europe and America millennialist Christian groups like the Templers and Millerites believed they had found in the Christian scriptures evidence supporting their conviction that history had ended and the return of Jesus Christ was at hand. In the Middle East, a markedly similar ferment developed around the belief that the fulfilment of various prophecies in the Qur'án and Islamic Traditions was imminent.

It was against this backdrop of expectations that a young descendent of the Prophet Muhammad, by the name of Siyyid 'Alí Muhammad, declared Himself to be a Messenger of God. He assumed the title of *Báb* or Gate. Like John the Baptist, He claimed to be the Herald of One greater than Himself. In preparation for the One Whom He called 'Him Whom God shall manifest', the Báb initiated new religious practices which replaced the old, outdated ones. He revealed prayers and laws providing His followers with insights into the spiritual and social requirements of a new age.

The story of the Báb is fascinating in its own right but too long to tell here. After eighteen people had spontaneously recognized the validity of His claim through dreams and visions, and had become His disciples, the Báb wrote a letter and instructed the first of His followers to deliver it to Bahá'u'lláh. The letter informed Him of the new Revelation. Upon receiving this missive from the Báb, Bahá'u'lláh immediately championed His Cause.

The years following the Báb's Declaration were filled with turmoil. In a single year the ferociously fanatical and ignorant Persian Muslims murdered four thousand adherents to His Cause. After only six years, the Báb's mission was complete and it was for His love of Bahá'u'lláh that He sacrificed His own life. At the time of the dramatic martyrdom of the Báb in the northern city of Tabríz in 1850, His followers were unaware that Bahá'u'lláh had been chosen to be 'Him Whom God shall manifest', the Messenger of God foretold by the Báb.

4·The Birth of the Baháʼí Revelation

Baháʼuʼlláh's given name was Mírzá Husayn ʻAlí, and the title of Bahá was adopted by Him during the time when He was a follower of the Báb. To break with the traditions of Islam, many of the followers of the Báb adopted non-Muslim names. In Arabic, *Bahá* means 'Glory', and later he was known to His followers as *Baháʼuʼlláh*, 'The Glory of God'.

Baháʼuʼlláh was born in Teheran, Persia on the 12th of November 1817 into a noble, respected and wealthy family. A career in government was open to Him as His father was a minister of state in the court of the King. However, Baháʼuʼlláh was not interested in politics, His kingdom was not of this world.

Baháʼuʼlláh's mission began in August 1852 in a subterranean dungeon in Teheran's notorious *Siyáh-Chál*, the 'Black Pit', where he was confined during the height of the persecution of the followers of the Báb. It was in this dungeon that Baháʼuʼlláh received His revelation. Every Messenger of God receives His revelation in a distinctive way: Moses was given the Commandments of God from a Burning Bush on the slopes of Mount Sinai; Jesus received the Holy Spirit in the form of a dove which descended upon Him while He was being baptized in the River Jordan; Muhammad was visited by the archangel Gabriel and given the *súrihs* of the Qurʼán.

Bahá'u'lláh described the moment of His revelation in an Epistle to the Persian King, Násiri'd-Dín Sháh, who had confined Him in the Black Pit of Teheran and then exiled Him from His native land:

> O King! I was but a man like others, asleep upon my couch, when lo, the breezes of the All-Glorious were wafted over Me, and taught Me the knowledge of all that hath been. This thing is not of Me, but from the One Who is Almighty and All-Knowing. He bade Me lift up My voice between earth and heaven, and for this there befell Me what hath caused the tears of every man of understanding to flow ... This is but a leaf which the winds of the will of Thy Lord, the Almighty, the All-Praised, have stirred ... His all-compelling summons hath reached Me, and caused Me to speak His praise amidst all people. I was indeed as one dead when His behest was uttered. The hand of the will of Thy Lord, the Compassionate, the Merciful, transformed Me. GPB:102

Bahá'u'lláh is being very generous and forgiving here in describing the floor of the dungeon into which the King had thrown Him as a 'couch'. Towards the end of His life, Bahá'u'lláh, writing about His early experiences, included a brief description of the conditions in the Black Pit:

> We were consigned for four months to a place foul beyond comparison. The dungeon was wrapped in thick darkness, and our fellow-prisoners numbered nearly a hundred and fifty souls: thieves, assassins and highwaymen. Though crowded, it had no other outlet than the passage by which We entered. Most of these men had neither clothes nor bedding to lie on. God alone knoweth what befell Us in that most foul-smelling and gloomy place. ESW:20–21

It was a cruel time for the followers of the Báb. Each day the guards would descend the three flights of stairs to the

Pit (the only way in or out of the dungeon), seize one or more of the prisoners and drag them out to be executed. In the streets of Teheran, Western observers were appalled by the scenes of the followers of the Báb being blown out of the mouths of cannons, hacked to death with axes and swords, and led to their deaths with burning candles inserted into wounds cut into their bodies. It was in these circumstances and faced with the prospect of His own imminent death that Bahá'u'lláh received the first intimation of His mission:

> During the days I lay in the prison of Teheran, though the galling weight of the chains and the stench-filled air allowed Me but little sleep, still in those infrequent moments of slumber I felt as if something flowed from the crown of My head over My breast, even as a mighty torrent that precipitateth itself upon the earth from the summit of a lofty mountain. ESW:22

> One night, in a dream, these exalted words were heard on every side: 'Verily, We shall render Thee victorious by Thyself and by Thy Pen. Grieve Thou not for that which hath befallen Thee, neither be Thou afraid, for Thou art in safety. Erelong will God raise up the treasures of the earth – men who will aid Thee through Thyself and through Thy name, wherewith God hath revived the hearts of such as have recognised Him.' ESW:21

5·THE EXILE

When people ask me about Bahá'u'lláh and I tell them that He spent nearly forty years of His life as a prisoner and an exile, they invariably ask me what He was imprisoned for. 'He must have done *something*,' they say. It is difficult if you live in a society where there are religious freedoms and civil rights to imagine what it is like to live in a time or place where a social standard of religious tolerance does not exist.

Whenever a Messenger of God comes and begins teaching new ideas, the people rise up against Him. This opposition usually originates from two sectors. Firstly the religious leaders see the birth of a new religion as a threat to their own. They are more concerned with their own power than considering the spiritual truths the Messenger is teaching. They oppose the Messenger because they cannot maintain control over the population if they begin to doubt their right to control their spiritual lives. The second source of opposition comes from the secular powers of the day, the kings and rulers who do their utmost to squash the birth of religions. Consider for a moment the histories of the other Messengers and recall what they had to withstand from the likes of Pharaoh and Herod Antipas during Their age.

Bahá'u'lláh was initially persecuted for being a supporter of the Báb and then when He received and revealed His own revelation, he was persecuted again. The religious leaders and the rulers of Persia tried to destroy the emerging religion in their midst. When they publicly executed the Báb, killed tens of thousands of His followers, and imprisoned most of the rest, they thought that they had succeeded.

Eventually, after four months, Bahá'u'lláh was released from the Black Pit, and still without trial or recourse He was immediately banished with His family from His native land. Although he could have gone north into Russia, Bahá'u'lláh instead chose banishment to neighbouring 'Iráq which was then under the rule of the Ottoman Empire. The Persian government confiscated His wealth and properties, and His family including His small children had to climb in the dead of winter through the snow-swept mountain passes between Persia and 'Iráq. He was never to return to Persia again.

This expulsion was the beginning of forty years of exile, imprisonment and bitter persecution. Upon His arrival in Baghdad, Bahá'u'lláh gave priority to the needs of the community of the followers of the Báb who had fled the persecution in their homeland. With the execution of the Báb and decimation of the leadership among His followers, Bahá'u'lláh found the community in Baghdad despondent and disorganized. Over the next ten years Bahá'u'lláh shaped and unified the community without informing them of the revelation He had received in the Black Pit. Steadily the fame and prestige of Bahá'u'lláh grew, not only among the followers of the teachings of the Báb, but among the general population of 'Iráq. Persian followers of the Báb began to arrive in Baghdad to seek the advice of Bahá'u'lláh, and then carried back encouraging letters and messages. The Islamic religious leaders of Baghdad became alarmed at the influence which this Persian exile had, and incited the Ottoman officials to remove Bahá'u'lláh farther away from Persia. Until He was finally ordered to leave Baghdad, Bahá'u'lláh continued preparing the followers of the Báb for the realization that the One Whom the Báb had foretold, had indeed come.

Some already recognized in the character of Bahá'u'lláh the One of Whom the Báb had written, but they saw that the time was not right to refer openly to Bahá'u'lláh as the Promised One. Bahá'u'lláh chose the occasion of His forced departure from Baghdad to declare that He was in fact 'Him Whom God shall manifest'.

Situated on the outskirts of Baghdad, across the River Tigris from the house where Bahá'u'lláh was held under house arrest, there was a garden where He assembled the band of followers who were going with him into exile in Constantinople, and also those who were to stay behind. Bahá'u'lláh named this garden Ridván, which means 'Paradise' in Arabic.

Over a period of twelve days Bahá'u'lláh made His public declaration of His mission, and informed the people present that the prophecies and promises of the Báb were fulfilled. Every year, this twelve-day period is commemorated during the Festival of Ridván, and the first, ninth and twelfth days of this festival are set aside as Holy Days. From this point forward the vast majority of the followers of the Báb turned to Bahá'u'lláh and became known as Bahá'ís. The exile which had begun when Bahá'u'lláh was forced to leave Teheran and which then led to Baghdad, was now set to continue to Constantinople, Adrianople, and finally to the prison city of 'Akká.

6·THE WRITINGS OF BAHÁ'U'LLÁH

We are privileged to live in the age of the written word. In previous ages, the words of the Messengers of God were most often passed down from generation to generation by word of mouth, becoming the oral tradition of a people until they were finally written down. The words of Jesus were recorded in the Gospels of the Bible by His disciples long after He had died. Jesus spoke to people and they remembered what He said. There is no indication that Jesus could read or write, nor did he need to. He was a teacher of men's hearts, and the principle means of communication in His lifetime was verbal.

In the Bahá'í Faith, meticulous effort has been made to gather together the writings of Bahá'u'lláh and preserve the original text written in His own hand. Bahá'ís are fortunate to have such authoritative texts to which to refer. This in itself will avoid the confusion which other religions have had to face in the past concerning what were or were not the actual words of the Messenger of God.

Bahá'u'lláh continued to write during His entire ministry while in prison and in exile. The sum total of His books, tablets, and epistles numbers more than a hundred volumes. He wrote most of them to specific individuals in response to questions asked of Him. Each missive was composed in the language and vocabulary the recipient understood and

35

within the literary style he would recognize. To the Islamic theologian, Bahá'u'lláh wrote in terms of Qur'ánic law and the traditions of the *hadith*; to the Christian clergyman, He employed biblical concepts and symbols; to the Súfí, He spoke in the style of mystic symbolism; to the political ruler, He chose direct and didactic words.

Regardless of their intended recipient, Bahá'u'lláh's books are at once personal and universal. They not only answered the enquirers' questions and satisfied their particular needs, but at the same time each missive reveals knowledge appropriate to all mankind. Bahá'u'lláh wrote within a wide spectrum of subjects: the history of religion, practical and applied ethics, morality, spirituality, economics, social organization, human rights, jurisprudence, the arts, metaphysics, science, mysticism, and prophecy.

Some of the better known works of Bahá'u'lláh include the following: the *Kalimát-i-Maknúnih (Hidden Words)* is unlike any other religious book, itself a new genre of literature. It is composed of 153 proverb-like utterances which beautifully present the depths of religious understanding in general, the spiritual truths at the heart of all religions. It is wisdom wrapped in brevity. It was revealed in two parts, the first in Arabic and the second in Persian, each language reflecting a style of literature and having a flavour all its own.

The *Haft-Vádí (Seven Valleys)* has been described as the summit of achievement in the realm of mystical composition. In this timeless and placeless description of the inner verities of religion, Bahá'u'lláh employs the terminology of the twelfth-century Súfí, Farídu'd-Dín 'Attár to describe the stages on the mystic path along which the seeker must travel towards God. These seven stages or valleys as Bahá'u'lláh refers to them are: the Valley of Search, the Valley of Love, the Valley of Knowledge, the Valley of Unity, the Valley of Contentment, the Valley of Wonderment, and the Valley of True Poverty and Absolute Nothingness.

The *Chihár-Vádí (Four Valleys)* is an epistle written in Baghdad, and like the *Seven Valleys* is a mystical composition in which Bahá'u'lláh describes the four ways in which the traces of the unseen God can be perceived, the four stages of the human heart, and the four kinds of mystic seeker in the quest for God.

The *Kitáb-i-Iqán (Book of Certitude)* presents the continuum of Divine revelation across the ages. It describes and affirms the common thread running through all religions.

The central book of the Bahá'í Faith is the *Kitáb-i-Aqdas (Most Holy Book)*. It is in this book that Bahá'u'lláh has outlined the laws and ordinances of this age.

> While in prison We have revealed a Book which We have entitled 'The Most Holy Book'. We have enacted laws therein and adorned it with the commandments of thy Lord Who exerciseth authority over all that are in the heavens and on the earth. Say: Take hold of it, O people, and observe that which hath been set down in it of the wondrous precepts of your Lord, the Forgiving, the Bountiful. It will truly prosper you both in this world and the next and will purge you of whatsoever ill beseemeth you. He is indeed the Ordainer, the Expounder, the Giver, the Generous, the Gracious, the All-Praised. TB:262

Some of Bahá'u'lláh's other books include: the *Bishárát (Glad Tidings)*, the *Kalimát-i-Fidawsíyyih (Words of Paradise)*, and the *Kitáb-i-'Ahd (Book of the Covenant)*. The *Lawh-i-Ibn-i-Dhi'b (Epistle to the Son of the Wolf)* was the last major volume revealed by Bahá'u'lláh. It was addressed to the son of the man who was instrumental in the execution of many Bahá'ís and whom Bahá'u'lláh had named 'The Wolf'. In it, Bahá'u'lláh summarizes the Bahá'í Revelation and quotes selected passages from His own writing.

7 · THE ANNOUNCEMENT TO THE KINGS

Bahá'u'lláh remained in the capital of the Ottoman Empire, Constantinople, now called Istanbul, for a period of four months before He was exiled again by the Turkish government to the city of Adrianople. Adrianople, known today as Edirne, was in the European part of Turkey on the border with Greece and Bulgaria. As a result of this latest exile, Bahá'u'lláh became the first Messenger of God in recorded history to have crossed from Asia into Europe.

It was during the next five years while He lived in Adrianople, that Bahá'u'lláh began to proclaim His message to the kings and rulers of the earth, and announced that He was the Promised One of all ages. One after the other, Bahá'u'lláh turned His attention to the crowned heads of Europe and Asia, inviting them to resolve their differences and work for the establishment of world peace. These included Napoleon III of France, Kaiser William I of Germany, Tzar Nicolaevitch Alexander II of Russia, Sultán 'Abdu'l - 'Azíz of the Ottoman Empire, Francis Joseph, Emperor of Austria and King of Hungary, Násiri'd-Dín Sháh of Persia, Pope Pius IX of the Roman Catholic Church, and Queen Victoria of the British Empire. Although He spoke to each one, discussing the specific strengths or weaknesses of their individual policies, He also proclaimed the appearance of a new Messenger of God and outlined the responsibilities of those in power to safeguard the well-being of all people and to use their resources for the establishment of international peace.

Bahá'u'lláh praised those who had promoted justice and human rights, and warned those who were heading towards disaster. He promised each one a glorious destiny if they listened to His counsel, and predicted the downfall of those who were heedless.

The fate of each one of these rulers is fascinating. Bahá'u'lláh first wrote to the most powerful monarch of the times, Napoleon III of France:

> O King of Paris! Tell the priest to ring the bells no longer. By God, the True One! The Most Mighty Bell hath appeared . . . We have desired for thee naught except that which is better for thee than what thou dost possess and all the treasures of the earth . . . Set your face towards Him [Bahá'u'lláh] on this Day which God hath exalted above all other days, and whereon the All-Merciful hath shed the splendour of His effulgent glory upon all who are in heaven and all who are on earth. Arise thou to serve God and help His Cause. He verily, will assist thee with the hosts of the seen and the unseen, and will set thee king over all that whereon the sun riseth . . . PB:17

Napoleon III is reported to have read Bahá'u'lláh's letter and thrown it over his shoulder, arrogantly declaring that 'If this is of God, I am two Gods.' Napoleon III was to receive two letters. Soon after the first, Bahá'u'lláh wrote again reminding him of the value of courtesy and compassion for the victims of oppression. Bahá'u'lláh offered him the opportunity of redeeming his past behaviour by heeding the advice of the Messenger of God, at the same time predicting the ruin of Napoleon III if he did not.

> O King! . . . Hadst thou been sincere in thy words, thou wouldst have not cast behind thy back the Book

of God . . . For what thou hast done, thy kingdom shall be thrown into confusion, and thine empire shall pass from thine hands, as a punishment for that which thou hast wrought. Then wilt thou know how thou hast plainly erred . . . Hath thy pomp made thee proud? By My Life! It shall not endure; nay, it shall soon pass away . . . We see abasement hastening after thee, whilst thou art of the heedless . . . PB:20

Napoleon III, who was the most illustrious Western monarch of his day, sustained a sudden and ignominious defeat at the battle of Sedan in 1870, an event which marked one of the greatest military surrenders in modern history. He lost his kingdom and spent the remaining years of his life in disgrace and exile. When the empire collapsed, his monarchy was replaced by the third French Republic. Napoleon III was the last king of France. Kaiser William I of Germany, the king who defeated him, was crowned Emperor of a united Germany in a ceremony which took place in the Palace of Versailles.

After the defeat of Napoleon III, Kaiser William I of Germany also received a tablet from Bahá'u'lláh:

Say: O King of Berlin! Give ear unto the Voice calling from this manifest Temple . . . Take heed lest pride debar thee from recognizing the Dayspring of Divine Revelation, lest earthly desires shut thee out, as by a veil, from the Lord of the Throne above and the earth below . . . Do thou remember the one whose power transcended thy power [Napoleon III], and whose station excelled thy station? Where is he? Whither are gone the things he possessed? Take warning, and be not of them that are fast asleep. He it was who cast the Tablet of God behind him, when we made known unto him what the host of tyranny had caused Us to suffer. Wherefore, disgrace assailed him from all sides, and he went down to dust in great loss. Think deeply, O King, concerning him, and concerning them who, like unto thee, have conquered cities and ruled over men. The All-Merciful brought them down from their palaces to their graves. Be warned, be of them who reflect . . . PB:39

Kaiser William I of Germany, the conqueror of Napoleon III, did not think deeply or reflect. He failed to heed the warning of the very specific consequences which lay ahead if Germany were not to begin the process of disarmament. Bahá'u'lláh concluded His tablet to William I with these prophecies:

O banks of the Rhine! We have seen you covered with gore, inasmuch as the swords of retribution were drawn against you; and you shall have another turn. And We hear the lamentations of Berlin, though she be today in conspicuous glory. PB:39

It was with these words that Bahá'u'lláh predicted the two great conflicts of the twentieth century, forty-four years before the First World War, and sixty-nine years before the Second. Kaiser William I himself sustained two attempts on his life, and his throne was bequeathed to his son. William II, through pride and short-sightedness, engulfed Europe in a war which, when Germany lost, precipitated a swift and sudden revolution in the German capital. There were indeed great 'lamentations' in Berlin. Communism appeared in several cities, the Kaiser and the princes of the German states abdicated, and the constitution of the Weimar Republic marked the extinction of the empire. In its turn the weakness of the republic and the social instability of the times soon facilitated the rise to power of Adolf Hitler and Nazism.

To the east, Tzar Nicolaevitch Alexander II of Russia, also received a letter from Bahá'u'lláh:

O Tzar of Russia! Incline thine ear unto the voice of God, the King, the Holy, and turn thou unto the Paradise . . . Arise thou amongst men in the name of this

all-compelling Cause, and summon, then, the nations
unto God . . . Blessed be the king whose sovereignty
hath withheld him not from his Sovereign, and who
hath turned unto God with his heart. PB:27

Nicolaevitch Alexander II, Tzar of Russia, also failed to heed
the call of Bahá'u'lláh and, after suffering several attempts on
his life, finally died at the hand of an assassin. The harsh
policy of repression which he initiated against his own people in the latter part of his reign, and which his successors
maintained, led eventually to the Bolshevik Revolution. The
people whom he and his heirs had oppressed finally rose
up and swept away the empire of the Tzars forever. They
executed the Tzar with his consort and family, and in so
doing extinguished the dynasty of the Romanoffs. A time of
war, disease and famine led to the establishment of a militant
proletariat government which, until very recently with the
collapse of Communism, oppressed the population in much
the same way as the Tzars had done.

Although condemned to the penal colony of 'Akká by
Sultán 'Abdu'l-'Azíz of the Ottoman Empire, Bahá'u'lláh
wrote to His captor advising:

Hearken, O King, to the speech of Him that speaketh
the truth, Him that doth not ask thee to recompense
Him with the things God hath chosen to bestow upon
thee, Him Who unerringly treadeth the straight Path. He
it is Who summoneth thee unto God, thy Lord, Who
showeth thee the right course, the way that leadeth to
true felicity, that haply thou mayest be of them with
whom it shall be well . . . Observe, O king, with thine
inmost heart and with thy whole being, the precepts of
God, and walk not in the paths of the oppressor . . .
Shouldst thou cause rivers of justice to spread their
waters amongst thy subjects, God would surely aid
thee with the hosts of the unseen and of the seen, and
would strengthen thee in thine affairs . . . Overstep not
the bounds of moderation, and deal justly with them
that serve thee. PB:47

Sultán 'Abdu'l-'Azíz was deposed after a palace revolution and assassinated in 1876. Forty-two years later, the First World War saw the final dissolution of the Ottoman Empire and the abolition of the sultanate which had endured for more than six centuries.

Bahá'u'lláh then turned his attention to Francis Joseph, the Emperor of Austria and King of Hungary, whom He counselled thus:

> O Emperor of Austria! . . . We have been with thee at all times, and found thee clinging unto the Branch and heedless of the Root . . . We grieve to see thee circle round Our Name, whilst unaware of Us, though We were before thy face. PB:43

Francis Joseph made no response and soon found himself engulfed by an ocean of misfortune and tragedy. After a brief and precarious existence the shrunken republic which had been built on the ruins of his vanished Holy Roman Empire was blotted out from the political map of Europe.

Bahá'u'lláh then wrote to Násiri'd-Dín Sháh of Persia, the very king who had imprisoned and exiled Him thirteen years earlier:

> O King! . . . Look upon this Youth, O King, with the eyes of justice; judge thou, then, with truth concerning what hath befallen Him . . . They that surround thee love thee for their own sakes, whereas this Youth loveth thee for thine own sake, and hath had no desire except to draw thee nigh unto the seat of grace, and to turn thee toward the right-hand of justice. PB:58

Even the forgiving nature of Bahá'u'lláh's words could not persuade Násiri'd-Dín Sháh to change his ways and be wary of those who surrounded him. The Persian King was dramatically assassinated while at prayer on the eve of a jubilee celebration designed to go down in history as the greatest day in the annals of the Persian nation. The fortunes of his dynastic house steadily declined with the scandalous and irresponsible misconduct of his successor, which rapidly led to the disappearance of Násiri'd-Dín Sháh's corrupt Qájár dynasty.

To the head of the Roman Catholic Church, Pope Pius IX, Bahá'u'lláh openly declared that the long-awaited return of Christ had taken place:

> O Pope! Rend the veils asunder. He Who is the Lord of Lords is come overshadowed with clouds . . . this is the day whereon the Rock [Peter] crieth out and shouteth . . . saying: 'Lo, the Father is come, and that which ye were promised in the Kingdom is fulfilled.' PB:83

Pope Pius IX paid no attention to this announcement of the event for which he and all the 290 Popes before him had fervently prayed for the last 1,870 years. He was too busy with the internal politics of the Church. He had called the cardinals to Rome for the First Vatican Council and was lobbying their support for his doctrine of Papal Infallibility. Just as the Judaic Patriarchs and the Jewish population failed to recognize their Messiah the first time Christ had appeared, so Pope Pius IX and the largest church in Christendom failed to notice His return. They had forgotten the prophecy of the thief in the night. During his long occupancy of the Holy See, Pope Pius IX experienced the virtual extinction of the Pope's temporal sovereignty and power. The Papacy was changed forever. He saw the dispossession of the Papal States and of Rome itself, over which the Papal flag had flown for a thousand years.

Bahá'u'lláh also addressed one of His tablets to Queen Victoria of the British Empire:

> O Queen in London! Incline thine ear unto the voice of thy Lord, the Lord of all mankind . . . God hath, truly, destined a reward for thee . . . He, verily, will pay the doer of good his due recompense . . . thou hast entrusted the reins of council into the hands of the representatives of the people. Thou, indeed, hast done well, for thereby the foundations of the edifice

of thine affairs will be strengthened, and the hearts of all that are beneath thy shadow, whether high or low, will be tranquillized. PB:33

Queen Victoria was the only monarch who responded without arrogance, conceit or silence. She is reported to have commented upon reading Bahá'u'lláh's letter: 'If this is of God, it will endure; if it is not, it can do no harm.' Queen Victoria was the longest reigning monarch in her country's history, and of all the kings and queens Bahá'u'lláh wrote to, it is perhaps more than a coincidence that her throne is the only one still occupied. One by one the others either refused or ignored His call. In their eyes, Bahá'u'lláh was a lowly and presumptuous prisoner of the Ottoman Empire who dared to give counsel to kings.

Bahá'u'lláh was offering them the opportunity to achieve what He called the 'Most Great Peace' – a condition of permanent peace and world unity to be founded on Bahá'u'lláh's principles and teachings. The Most Great Peace would signal the coming of age and maturity of mankind, but the kings and rulers failed to gather together to resolve their differences. Had they begun the process of disarmament then in the latter part of the nineteenth century, the world would have been spared all the death and destruction of the wars we have seen in the twentieth century.

After the kings and rulers had failed to respond to His call, Bahá'u'lláh, in place of the Most Great Peace, offered them instead a 'Lesser Peace':

O Kings of the earth! We see you increasing every year your expenditures, and laying the burden thereof on your subjects. This, verily, is wholly and grossly unjust. Fear the sighs and tears of this Wronged One, and lay not excessive burdens on your peoples. Do not rob them to rear palaces for yourselves; nay rather choose for them that which ye choose for yourselves. Thus We unfold to your eyes that which profiteth you, if ye but perceive. Your people are your treasures. Beware lest your rule violate the commandments of God, and ye

45

deliver your wards to the hands of the robber. By them ye rule, by their means ye subsist, by their aid ye conquer. Yet, how disdainfully ye look upon them! How strange, how very strange!

Now that ye have refused the Most Great Peace, hold ye fast unto this, the Lesser Peace, that haply ye may in some degree better your own condition and that of your dependants.

O rulers of the earth! Be reconciled among yourselves, that ye may need no more armaments save in a measure to safeguard your territories and dominions. Beware lest ye disregard the counsel of the All-Knowing, the Faithful.

Be united, O kings of the earth, for thereby will the tempest of discord be stilled amongst you, and your people find rest, if ye be of them that comprehend. PB:12

We can now witness in the world around us the process towards a Lesser Peace. Although a step in the right direction, the Lesser Peace is still just a political truce, in which the nations of the world try to bring about an end to war and open conflict without substantially changing their basic self-serving mentality. Little by little the nuclear weapons will be destroyed and strategic armaments reduced, but this is not a solution. If the bombs are taken away but the people's hearts are not changed, they will still think in terms of weapons. Anything can be used as a weapon: finance, technology, international trade, natural resources, even food. Until the root causes of war are eradicated, we will always be potentially at war, even though we are not fighting.

Bahá'ís believe we must strive for the equality of gender and races, and work to reduce the disparate extremes between rich and poor. Only when we have eliminated the prejudice and avarice we hold within us, will the Lesser Peace evolve into the Most Great Peace.

In the following words, Bahá'u'lláh describes the station of any monarch who heeds His call:

How great is the blessedness that awaiteth the king who will arise to aid My Cause in My Kingdom, who will detach himself from all else but Me! PB:6

Nearly seventy years after Queen Victoria received the letter from Bahá'u'lláh, one of her granddaughters, the Dowager Queen Marie of Rumania, accepted the Cause of Bahá'u'lláh in the latter part of her life and became a supporter of the Bahá'í Faith. And exactly one hundred years after Bahá'u'lláh's proclamation to the kings of the earth, the first reigning monarch embraced the Bahá'í Faith – in 1968, after many months of investigating the teachings of Bahá'u'lláh, His Highness Malietoa Tanumafili II of the Pacific nation of Western Samoa, became a Bahá'í.

8·BAHÁ'U'LLÁH'S ARRIVAL IN THE HOLY LAND

As had happened in Baghdad and Constantinople, the fame of Bahá'u'lláh grew wherever the government sent Him. People would flock around the house where He was confined, seeking to hear the voice or behold the face of the Messenger of God. Finally the Turkish government decided that even Adrianople was too close to the capital, and exiled Bahá'u'lláh to the most remote outpost of the Ottoman Empire.

The place they chose for his next banishment was the fortress-city of 'Akká. This penal colony was notorious for the foulness of its climate and its many diseases. It was a place reserved for the incarceration of the most dangerous of criminals, a prison in which people were not expected to live very long. So bad was the very air that it was said that if a bird flew over the city of 'Akká it would fall down dead from the stench. The members of Bahá'u'lláh's family, together with a company of His followers, were exiled with Him.

For the next two years and two months, Bahá'u'lláh would be held in the fortress citadel itself under the strictest of orders to isolate Him from visitors and from the general populace. Bahá'ís, nevertheless, continued to arrive from distant provinces and nations, seeking to be near Him. It

The Prison of 'Akká

was during this particularly difficult period of Bahá'u'lláh's imprisonment that all pilgrims were turned away heart-broken without seeing Him; but this condition changed in a remarkable way.

One extremely hot night, one of Bahá'u'lláh's sons, Mírzá Mihdí, fell through a skylight while pacing the roof of the prison rapt in prayer. He fell on to some crates which mortally wounded him. Bahá'u'lláh found His son conscious and offered to save his life but, instead of asking to be healed, Mírzá Mihdí's dying wish to his Father was for his life to be accepted as a ransom for those who were prevented from entering Bahá'u'lláh's presence. He asked his Father to accept the sacrifice of his life so that the pilgrims who had come from so far could meet, face to face, the Messenger of God. Bahá'u'lláh granted His dying son's request, and Mírzá Mihdí was buried just outside the prison walls. Bahá'u'lláh frequently praised His son's selflessness and spirituality in His writings.

Very soon after the death of His son, Bahá'u'lláh's restricted confinement was lessened and He was allowed to live under house arrest in a nearby building. Miraculously, the guards at the gates of the prison city began to allow Bahá'í visitors through.

For a long time the exiles were shunned by the superstitious local population who had been warned in public sermons against 'the God of the Persians'. Life was very difficult for the small band of exiles, several of whom died as the result of the privations and other conditions to which they were subjected.

9·THE PASSING OF BAHÁ'U'LLÁH

After many years within the walls of 'Akká, Bahá'u'lláh was permitted to leave the prison and live nearby in a place called Bahjí. Today Bahjí is surrounded by beautiful gardens through which Bahá'í pilgrims and visitors walk as they approach Bahá'u'lláh's resting place. Aside from the gardens, Bahjí has been kept as it was during Bahá'u'lláh's final years. Inside the house one can see where He and His family lived, the room where Bahá'u'lláh received numerous early Bahá'ís and visiting dignitaries, including Edward Granville Browne, and the room where He died.

Bahá'u'lláh died at Bahjí on the 29th of May 1892, in His seventy-fifth year. At the time of His passing, the Cause which had been entrusted to Him during His imprisonment in the Black Pit had begun to spread far beyond the Islamic lands where it had taken shape, and it was beginning to be established in America, Europe and the rest of the world.

Bahá'u'lláh had appointed his eldest son, 'Abdu'l-Bahá (1844–1921) as His successor and the authorized interpreter of His writings. 'Abdu'l-Bahá, who since the age of eight had accompanied his Father in his imprisonments and exiles, sent the news of Bahá'u'lláh's passing to the Sultán of the Ottoman Empire, in a telegram which began with the words: 'The sun of Bahá has set . . .'

On the day of His passing, many notable personages,

among them Shí'ah and Sunní Moslems, Christians, Jews, and Druzes, as well as poets, religious leaders and government officials, began to arrive, lamenting the loss of Bahá'u'lláh and magnifying His virtues and greatness. For several weeks tributes and eulogies continued to arrive, in both verse and prose, in Arabic and Turkish, in the form of telegrams and letters. Even though the kings of the earth had ignored Bahá'u'lláh during His lifetime, countless thousands in Persia, India, Russia, 'Iráq, Turkey, Sudan, Palestine, Egypt and Syria had recognized Him as a Messenger of God.

During this first century since Bahá'u'lláh's passing, His followers have spread to every country, territory and island of the world. They have constantly, year after year, grown in number and remained united. The year 1992 is the centenary of Bahá'u'lláh's passing and has been declared a Holy Year in which Bahá'ís will dedicate their time to studying His writings and finding ways to implement His teachings and principles for the solution of the world's problems.

Bahá'u'lláh's vision of humanity united as one people, and His promise of the earth becoming a peaceful and common homeland to all mankind is as timely now as it was a hundred years ago. Now more than ever Bahá'ís are focusing on Bahá'u'lláh's message as the sole hope for humanity.

PART 3
THE BASIC TEACHINGS

10·GOD AND THE PURPOSE OF HUMAN LIFE

God was, is, and always will be beyond the knowledge of mankind. Just as the created can never fathom the creator, so humans, although striving to understand more and more of creation, can never comprehend God.

> God . . . is immeasurably above the understanding of all created things, and is exalted beyond the grasp of the minds of men. GWB:XXVI

In His writings, Bahá'u'lláh reaffirms the singularity of God, a truth which it has taken some cultures longer to acknowledge than others. With the diversity of languages and customs in the world, it is understandable how people in the past were unable to recognize their God in the forms of worship of others. The name of God has varied from language to language, from people to people, and from time to time, around the world. For some, their particular name for God became an exclusive possession marking themselves as elite and religiously superior, and this has led throughout history to many internecine conflicts.

Thankfully, we now live in more enlightened times. We can now see that the Hebrew *Yahweh* or *Jehovah*, the Arabic

Allah, the Korean *Shin*, the Spanish *Dios*, the English *God*, and even, in the African language of the Ntumu, *Zamba*, all refer to the same Supreme Being Whose reality transcends names. We are beginning to acknowledge that no one group of people is more spiritually blessed than any other. Despite our linguistic, cultural and historical differences, everyone is equal in the sight of God.

Bahá'u'lláh explains that the creation is separate from the Creator. However, throughout all of creation are the traces of God's work. The majestic swirl of the stars and planets of our galaxy and the very atoms of which they are composed reflect the awesome and awe-inspiring workmanship of the Creator. The existence of the universe and the dynamic processes which govern the appearance of life itself are sufficient proof of their having emanated from the Divine Will. God is the Creator not only of the complex physical interaction of forces seen at work in nature, but also of more subtle planes of existence, dimensions unseen by human eyes, whose existence lies beyond the perception of senses and mind, a non-physical cosmos which interacts with our spiritual nature. These dimensions constitute a greater reality than the physical universe.

> He is really a believer in the Unity of God who recognizes in each and every created thing the sign of the revelation of Him Who is the Eternal Truth, and not he who maintaineth that the creature is indistinguishable from the Creator. GWB:XCIII

For the individual, the purpose of our creation is to know and love God. Throughout the Bahá'í Holy Scriptures, God is spoken of in attributes rather than descriptions: the All-Knowing, the All-Wise, the Ever-Forgiving, the Most Generous, the Almighty, the All-Glorious, the Most-Bountiful. These Divine qualities are expressed in words whose basic meanings lie within the grasp of human understanding but which can only be alluded to within the limits of language. We can never evolve a spiritual vocabulary adequate to describe the attributes of God. The use of these attributive terms within the writings of Bahá'u'lláh clearly demonstrates that God is beyond the notions of shape and form, above the concepts of race and gender. This existence is without location or condition, an unknowable essence which cannot be made anthropomorphic. God is not created in our image; we are created in the likeness of God. That ethereal part of us, our spiritual reality, is this Divine image.

Humans are essentially spiritual beings with outward bodies which change shape and size throughout the course of our lives, but whose inner being remains unaffected and continues to progress regardless of the condition of the physical vehicle which contains it. Collectively as a species, human beings have always been endowed with souls and the potential to acknowledge the existence of our Creator, regardless of the particular form our bodies have assumed throughout the continuum of our material existence. We are soul-bearing entities whose *raison d'être* has always been to know and love God.

> The purpose of God in creating man hath been, and will ever be, to enable him to know his Creator and to attain His Presence. To this most excellent aim, this supreme objective, all the heavenly Books and the divinely-revealed and weighty Scriptures unequivocally bear witness. GWB:XXIX

The lifespan of our physical existence is infinitesimal when compared to the infinite expanse and duration of the universe around us. Our life here on earth is but a fleeting moment and only a small part of the reason why God created us. Knowing and loving God is an eternal process which continues after this life. Within each of us there exists a spiritual aspect which is suited to that eternal process; it is deathless and part of an unseen spiritual dimension. The entire physical universe is encompassed and pervaded by this spiritual dimension – an infinity within an infinity.

11·THE NATURE OF
LIFE AFTER DEATH

Life after death has always been described by analogy. The soul and eternal life can neither be defined in absolute terms like the physical phenomena of this world, nor explained in conditional terms like abstract concepts. They are neither tangible realities nor intellectual abstractions, and because of the limitation of our experience their existence can only be alluded to. Intimation is perhaps the only way to describe things which are metaphysical in nature.

It is a descriptive problem common to all religions throughout the ages. The Messengers of God in each age have employed in Their Holy Scriptures analogies of things familiar to the people of Their times. As times changed, however, so did the analogies. The comparisons of Moses were simple and direct, while Christ chose to teach His followers using parables, a special form of narrative analogy with hidden spiritual meanings. In this age, Bahá'u'lláh has written:

Know, verily, that the soul is a sign of God, a heavenly gem whose reality the learned of men hath failed to grasp, and whose mystery no mind, however acute, can ever hope to unravel. It is the first among all created things to declare the excellence of its Creator, the first to recognize His glory, to cleave to His

truth, and to bow down in adoration before Him.
GWB:LXXXII

The soul is the ultimate reality of the individual; it is one's true identity. The body and mind are the instruments of our individual physical and intellectual existence, but the soul transcends their limitations and possesses abilities which the others do not. Among these is the potential to recognize the existence and glory of God. On this physical and ephemeral plane of existence, however, the body and mind are necessary to the process of our spiritual development. This life is a preparation for what is to come after death, just as our pre-natal existence within the womb was a preparation for this life:

> The world beyond is as different from this world as this world is different from that of the child while still in the womb of its mother. GWB:LXXXI

The purpose of something is often best seen in retrospect. This is evident when the following two questions are compared: What was the purpose of the time spent in the womb of our mother? and: What is the purpose of this life? Hindsight makes the former question easier to answer than the latter. That 36- to 40-week period of gestation was a preparation for our survival in this world. By analogy, the time we spend in this world is the gestation period for our birth into the next.

The parallel is useful in understanding why preparation is necessary to progress. In the womb of our mother, we lived in a self-contained and personal universe. It was small but sufficient in size to provide everything we needed for our existence; we had the sustaining warmth from our mother's body, the nutrition and oxygen we acquired through the placenta and umbilical cord, but above all we had the constant love and attention of our mother. Now that we are here in this world, it is not difficult to see that the purpose of that existence was to grow. However, this understanding is only possible because we can now look back. While we were in the womb, it was not so clear. Most of the things we were growing were of no real use to us in the confined and limited world of the womb. We were developing legs in a place where there was nowhere to walk; lungs in an airless aquatic world of amniotic fluid; eyes and ears in a place less than ideal for sights and sounds. It was not until after we were born that these limbs and organs became useful. Aside from this, we were not even aware that we were growing these faculties. In fact, if we were conscious of their existence at all, they would have been mysterious and alien because there was no way we could even have guessed their function and future value. Had we been given the choice, we might have decided not to grow them because we could not understand their use. Imagine how handicapped we would later have been in this world.

Continuing the analogy, this world is the womb of the next, and its purpose is to provide us with an environment conducive to a different kind of growth. What we are growing, so to speak, are those spiritual senses and abilities which we will need in the next world. These faculties are spiritual in nature – attributes of the soul such as the ability to love, to show kindness, to be selfless – attributes which adorn our soul as our limbs adorn our bodies. These are the spiritual qualities we take with us into the next world when we die. Just because on this earthly plane of existence we cannot fully recognize their worth, we should not neglect those things which are conducive to their growth.

Spiritual neglect can cause the soul to be hindered in its development, just as insufficient nutrition can stunt the physical growth of the unborn child. Prayer, meditation, obedience to the laws of God, and service to humanity are some of the spiritual nutrients of the soul. The question arises as to what happens in the afterlife if the soul is neglected in this life. In this life the progress of the soul is dependent upon the will of the individual; in the life beyond, progress continues by the Will of God.

With this in mind, it is understandable that Bahá'ís see eternal life as having already begun. Eternal life is not something that begins at death. Conception, birth, life, and death are all stages along a spiritual continuum. Our true reality emanates from our eternal Creator and from the moment of our conception; humans are both physical and spiritual beings already on the pathway of eternity. Carried by our body in this world and then joyously set free, the soul passes from one state of existence to the next on its journey back to God. This immortal part of our being is the repository of unseen faculties. The soul is mysterious in nature; in this life we only have an inkling of its abilities. Bahá'u'lláh further explains:

> Verily I say, the human soul is exalted above all egress and regress. It is still, and yet it soareth; it moveth, and yet it is still. It is, in itself, a testimony that beareth witness to the existence of a world that is contingent, as well as to the reality of a world that hath neither beginning nor end. Behold how the dream thou hast dreamed is, after the lapse of many years, re-enacted before thine eyes. Consider how strange is the mystery of the world that appeareth to thee in thy dream. Ponder in thine heart upon the unsearchable wisdom of God, and meditate on its manifold revelations . . .
> GWB:LXXXII

The paradox of the dreaming state in which sequence and distance are not restricted as they are in the waking state and the interaction between the two, is given as an analogy of the limitless nature of the soul. The physical universe, at least on the level at which we function within it, is bounded by four dimensions: three spatial and one temporal. Physical things, including our material selves, exist with height, breadth and depth, and at a particular moment in time. As with the subconscious mind in the dreaming state, the soul, together with the spiritual eternity in which it exists, is not limited by these four dimensions of our contingent world.

Our realization of the nature of the soul must embrace a concept of both physical and spiritual paradox. Within the physical universe, perceptually we will always find our-selves at the midway point between the microcosm and the macrocosm. Within us is folded the universe of molecules, atoms and subatomic particles which are infinitely smaller than humans, and at the same time, we as humans are enwrapped within the universe of a stellar system, galaxies and things infinitely larger than ourselves. The soul exists within and beyond this physical cosmology, in spiritual dimensions we cannot perceive from the limited vantage point of this earthly life. The human soul is endowed with potentialities which will only later become manifest. Again by analogy, just as the double-helix structured DNA in our cells carries the genetic code of physical life, so the soul somehow carries the spiritual code of our eternal existence.

Because of the evanescent nature of physical life, we must not become attached to the material world or forget we have a soul. Referring to the soul, Bahá'u'lláh explains:

> If it be faithful to God, it will reflect His light, and will, eventually, return unto Him. If it fail, however, in its allegiance to its Creator, it will become a victim to self and passion, and will, in the end sink in their depths. GWB:LXXXII

This message of detachment is ancient to religious teachings. The writings of Bahá'u'lláh repeatedly remind us that the soul is our most precious possession, and Bahá'ís are exhorted to remain undistracted by the material world:

> He is not to be numbered with the people of Bahá who followeth his mundane desire, or fixeth his heart on things of the earth. He is My true follower who, if he come to a valley of pure gold, will pass straight through it aloof as a cloud, and will neither turn back, nor pause. GWB:LX

Our knowledge of the existence of God and our understanding of the nature of the soul and eternal life have grown over the ages, as mankind has progressed from one stage to another in the ongoing process of our collective spiritual evolution.

12·THE CONCEPT OF PROGRESSIVE REVELATION

The process of mankind's spiritual evolution continues because God sends Messengers from time to time. These Messengers are the means of humanity's development and progress throughout the ages; it is they who are responsible for our periodic elevation from a lesser to a greater degree of understanding regarding the existence and purpose of God. In fact, the only way people can know of God's purpose for us is through the Messengers He sends. These Messengers, or Manifestations of God as Bahá'u'lláh calls them, are the spiritual teachers of mankind. They educate the souls and minds of humanity and provide us with both spiritual and social guidance. Every thousand years or so, they appear and supply mankind with the teachings required for that age. They come one after another as teachers belonging to the same long-term educational process. Bahá'u'lláh refers to this process as Progressive Revelation:

> Contemplate with thine inward eye the chain of successive Revelations . . . I testify before God that each one of these Manifestations hath been sent down through the operation of the Divine Will and Purpose, that each hath been the bearer of a specific Message, that

each hath been entrusted with a divinely-revealed Book and been commissioned to unravel the mysteries of a mighty Tablet. The measure of the Revelation with which every one of them hath been identified had been definitely fore-ordained. GWB:XXXI

These Messengers raise the level of our spiritual understanding by revealing God's words, and each time they appear they fill the world with fresh spiritual impetus and advance mankind another step forward. Progressive Revelation is more than an educative process, it is part of the eternal covenant of Abraham in which God promised never to abandon mankind. In fulfilment of that covenant God has sent Krishna, Moses, Zoroaster, Buddha, Christ, Muhammad, the Báb and, most recently, Bahá'u'lláh.

Each of these Messengers brought a message appropriate to the time and place in which He appeared. His Dispensation, the sum-total of the teachings the Messenger has dispensed to mankind, is perfectly suited to that stage of our spiritual development:

Know of a certainty that in every Dispensation the light of Divine Revelation hath been vouchsafed unto men in direct proportion to their spiritual capacity. Consider the sun. How feeble its rays the moment it appeareth above the horizon. How gradually its warmth and potency increase as it approacheth the zenith, enabling meanwhile all created things to adapt themselves to the growing intensity of its light. How steadily it declineth until it reacheth its setting point. Were it, all of a sudden, to manifest the energies latent within it, it would, no doubt, cause injury to all created things . . . In like manner, if the Sun of Truth were suddenly to reveal, at the earliest stages of its manifestation, the full measure of the potencies which the providence of the Almighty hath bestowed upon it, the earth of human understanding would waste away and be consumed; for men's hearts would neither sustain the intensity of its revelation, nor be able to mirror forth the radiance of its

Bahá'í House of Worship, Kampala, Uganda

light. Dismayed and overpowered, they would cease to exist. GWB:XXXVIII

Progressive Revelation is an eternal process extending backwards into times before there were written records; and because of the antiquity of some of these Revelations, the names of the Messengers Themselves have been lost. Within the period of time for which we do have historical records, there is evidence of this process. As with our understanding of the purpose of our physical existence, Progressive Revelation is easier to understand in retrospect. The process of sequential Divine messages is not new to religious understanding. However, which of the Messengers a particular religion chooses to acknowledge is a matter of geography and chronology.

Throughout recorded history, many of the Messengers of God have arisen in that part of the Asian continent which extends from the shores of the Red and Mediterranean Seas in the West to the mouth of the River Ganges in the East. This part of the planet has been the birthplace of most of the world's religions. The western part of this region has a great religious tradition which has witnessed a long succession of Messengers. However, because of the chronology, the followers of each religion only recognize the Ones Who came before their particular Messenger. For example, Judaism acknowledges both Abraham and Moses; Christianity recognizes Abraham, Moses and then Christ; Islam identifies the succession of Abraham, Moses, Christ and then Muhammad.

Each of these religions has understood something of the process of Progressive Revelation but failed to see that it extends forwards as well as backwards into time. The Bahá'í Faith sees within its spiritual heritage all the Messengers of the past and recognizes Bahá'u'lláh as the most recent; but it also acknowledges that He will not be the last. To ensure that the succession of Messengers continues and that mankind is able to recognize them each time They appear, each One fulfils the prophecies of the previous Messengers and in turn foretells the coming of the next. In like manner, Bahá'u'lláh promises that another Messenger will come after Him, but not for at least a thousand years. Progressive Revelation is an eternal process forward. As long as there are human beings, God will continue to send His Messengers to guide our progress.

Each individual has the twin responsibilities of accepting the Messenger of God for the age in which he or she lives, and to follow the teachings that the Messenger brings. These teachings are found in the Sacred Scripture of each of the Messengers. In the times in which we live, the writings of Bahá'u'lláh provide us with the guidance we need in this age. His teachings contain primarily two kinds of guidance – spiritual and social – and take the form of laws and basic principles.

13·THE BASIC PRINCIPLES OF THE BAHÁ'Í FAITH

Spiritual teachings are universal and eternal. The Golden Rule, that epigraph which states that we should do unto others as we would have them do unto us, is ancient and found among the sayings of all the Messengers of God. Bahá'u'lláh in this age reminds us:

> O Son of Being! Ascribe not to any soul that which thou wouldst not have ascribed to thee, and say not that which thou doest not. This is My command unto thee, do thou observe it. AHW:29

Each time a Messenger appears, He reminds us of the spiritual nature of our true existence and prescribes attitudes of mind which are conducive to our spiritual growth. As with the process of Progressive Revelation, the spiritual teachings are likewise progressive and our understanding of them expands with the appearance of each new Messenger. These spiritual teachings are the threads which connect all the world religions. Spiritual guidance is universal to all times and places. Like the Messengers of the past, Bahá'u'lláh reiterates and augments these eternal spiritual verities in His writings by reminding us that:

Thine eye is My trust, suffer not the dust of vain desires
to becloud its lustre. Thine ear is a sign of My Bounty,
let not the tumult of unseemly motives turn it away
from My Word that encompasseth all creation. Thine
heart is My treasury, allow not the treacherous hand
of self to rob thee of the pearls which I have treasured
therein. Thine hand is a symbol of My loving-kindness,
hinder it not from holding fast unto My guarded and
hidden Tablets ... Unasked, I have showered upon
thee My grace. Unpetitioned, I have fulfilled thy wish.
In spite of thy undeserving, I have singled thee out for
My richest, My incalculable favours ... GWB:CLII

The followers of Bahá'u'lláh have several obligations which
promote the individual's spiritual growth and development.
In addition to daily prayer and reading from the Sacred
Writings each morning and evening, Bahá'ís fast from sunrise to sunset, abstaining from both food and drink, each
year during the nineteen-day fasting period. This spiritual
obligation begins at the age of fifteen and continues until the
age of seventy.

Spiritual teachings provide insight into the inner realities
and help to educate the soul of the individual, but these
represent only half of the guidance given by each Messenger
of God. Their social teachings address the outer realities and
assist in the education of society. These social teachings
often change with the coming of each Messenger, some of the
previous laws being maintained while others are abrogated
and replaced by new ones which suit the developmental and
social needs of the time.

The style and form of these spiritual and social teachings
have varied from age to age, but the message remains the
same. At one time the people of the world responded with
compliant and unquestioning obedience to the teachings
given to them by Moses in the Ten Commandments, whereas
in this day and age we are given guidance in the form of
injunctions which are often accompanied by an authoritative explanation or exegesis provided by the Messenger
Himself.

It is a sign of our collective progress towards social maturity that blind faith and fearful obedience have now been replaced by the kind of perceptive faith and loving obedience which spring from insight and understanding. Mankind has matured from a time in which we were instructed primarily with prohibitions. There are very few 'thou shalt not's' in the Bahá'í Faith; there are far more affirmative exhortations. For example, Bahá'ís are exhorted to associate with the followers of all religions with fellowship; to honour their parents; to study such arts and sciences as will benefit mankind; to distinguish themselves through good deeds; to be truthful, trustworthy and faithful; to be just and fair; to be tactful and wise; to be courteous, hospitable, persevering, detached, and closely united.

However, Bahá'u'lláh does prohibit His followers from those things which are personally and socially destructive. Bahá'ís are admonished to abstain from alcohol and drugs, aside from their prescriptive use in remedies by a physician. These substances impede the process of clear thinking and, what is more, their abuse is at the root of many diseases of the body and mind, to say nothing of their social harms. Gambling is also forbidden, for it ignites an obsessive addiction to materialism within the heart of the temporary winner and ultimately brings ruin to the eventual loser. Premarital and extramarital sexual relationships are likewise prohibited, reserving the intimacy of sexual intercourse as the appropriate expression of one's love and commitment within marriage. However, the strongest prohibition which Bahá'u'lláh delivers in His writings is against backbiting and calumny:

> O Son of Being! How couldst thou forget thine own faults and busy thyself with the faults of others? Whoso doeth this is accursed of Me. O Son of Man! Breathe not the sins of others so long as thou art thyself a sinner. Shouldst thou transgress this command, accursed wouldst thou be, and to this I bear witness. AHW:27–28

Bahá'ís recognize these as among the major social ailments

70

of our times. Contemporary society has somehow legiti-
mized the practice of subtle misrepresentation, derision
and fault-finding behind someone's back in both the spoken
and written word. It has become such an insidious social
habit that it pervades our conversations and the pages of
our newspapers and magazines. Bahá'ís are admonished by
Bahá'u'lláh to avoid backbiting and slander, and to strive
to attain a mentality which promotes unity and which
genuinely seeks to find the good qualities in others.

Bahá'u'lláh's teachings which address many other issues
and provide a wide-ranging source of guidance for both
the spiritual and practical aspects of daily life, may be
summarized in the basic principles of the Bahá'í Faith
outlined below.

There is only one God, and all the Messengers of the past
have come from Him in a continuous process of Progressive
Revelation. In addition to this, as Bahá'u'lláh points out, we
are all members of one global family:

It is not for him to pride himself who loveth his own
country, but rather for him who loveth the whole world.
The earth is but one country, and mankind its citizens.
GWB:CXVII

People should strive to eliminate all forms of prejudice.
Equality should be extended to everyone regardless of gender, race, religion, culture, age, heritage, language, occupa-
tion, social status, or their group's numerical strength:

Observe equity in your judgement, ye men of understanding heart! He that is unjust in his judgement is
destitute of the characteristics that distinguish man's
station. He Who is the Eternal Truth knoweth well what
the hearts of men conceal. GWB:C

An understanding of the importance of justice is fundamental to the progress of the individual's soul, and paramount
to the advancement of the society at large:

O Son of Spirit! The best beloved of all things in My sight is Justice; turn not away therefrom if thou desirest Me, and neglect it not in that I may confide in thee. By its aid thou shalt see with thine own eyes and not through the eyes of others, and thou shalt know of thine own knowledge and not through the knowledge of thy neighbour. Ponder this in thy heart; how it behooveth thee to be. Verily justice is My gift to thee and the sign of My loving-kindness. Set it then before thine eyes. AHW:2

The injustices of starvation and deprivation arise from a lack of conscience in the hearts of men and women. Poverty and the dire economic problems which face mankind must be solved on both a practical and spiritual level. To be effective, the solution must come from a sense of collective and personal responsibility. Bahá'u'lláh writes:

O Children of Dust! Tell the rich of the midnight sighing of the poor, lest heedlessness lead them into the path of destruction, and deprive them of the Tree of Wealth. To give and be generous are attributes of Mine; well is it with him that adorneth himself with My virtues . . . O Ye Rich Ones on Earth! The poor in your midst are My trust; guard ye My trust, and be not intent only on your own ease. PHW:49, 54

To achieve this, education must play a principal rôle. Education should be universal and appropriate, for it is the key which unlocks the doors to both individual and social progress. It is the duty of parents and the community to enable children to actualize that potential through education:

Man is the supreme Talisman. Lack of a proper education hath, however, deprived him of that which he doth inherently possess. Through a word proceeding out of the mouth of God he was called into being; by one word more he was guided to recognize the Source of his education; by yet another word his station and destiny were safeguarded. The Great Being saith: Regard man as a mine rich in gems of inestimable value. Education can, alone, cause it to reveal its treasures, and enable mankind to benefit therefrom. GWB:CXXII

It is time that educational institutions presented scientific and religious perspectives in such a way that they are not seen as conflicting. Science and religion should not be in opposition to each other, but rather recognized as different ways of describing the same phenomena. Teachers and parents should teach their children that there cannot logically be two conflicting explanations for the same thing. Both the analytic reasoning of scientific thought and the ethical morality of religious insight are needed in this age to promote an ever-advancing civilization.

The world has several basic needs to fulfil before it can move towards a global civilization. To secure the establishment and maintenance of world peace there should be created a commonwealth of nations with an effective international tribunal for settling disputes peacefully, a common world currency, a common system of weights and measures. Together these constitute the beginnings of the New World Order envisioned by Bahá'u'lláh over a hundred years ago:

The time must come when the imperative necessity for the holding of a vast, an all-embracing assemblage of men will be universally realized. The rulers and kings of the earth must needs attend it, and, participating in its deliberations, must consider such ways and means as will lay the foundation of the world's Great Peace amongst men. Such a peace demandeth that the great powers should resolve, for the sake of the tranquillity of the peoples of the earth, to be fully reconciled among themselves. Should any king take up arms against another, all should unitedly arise and prevent him. If this be done, the nations of the world will no longer require any armaments, except for the purpose of preserving the security of their realms and of maintaining internal order within their territories.

This will ensure the peace and composure of every people, government and nation. We fain would hope that the kings and rulers of the earth, the mirrors of the gracious and almighty name of God, may attain unto this station, and shield mankind from the onslaught of tyranny. GWB:CXVII

As a major feature of this New World Order, there needs to be selected either an existing or an artificial language to serve as an international auxiliary language, which would be taught in every school throughout the world alongside the native language and literature of that country:

The day is approaching when all the peoples of the world will have adopted one universal language and one common script. When this time is achieved, to whatsoever city a man may journey, it shall be as if he were entering his own home. GWB:CXVII

These basic principles have one common aspect: unity. This unity, however, does not mean uniformity. The sharing of things in common on a worldwide basis, such as a general system of weights and measures, one international unit of currency, and a universal auxiliary language, constitute elements of the planetization of mankind, but within this, the cultural identity and diversity of individuals must be protected, respected and valued as integral to the whole. This unity is the hub of Bahá'u'lláh's teachings. These principles are given to us by the Messenger of God to facilitate the coming together of all mankind. This is a stage in our development which will be recognized in the future as the beginning of the maturity of mankind.

14·THE PROCESS OF AN EVER-ADVANCING CIVILIZATION

Just as the individual purpose of life is to know and love God, so, for human society as a whole, the purpose of life is to promote an ever-advancing civilization. Each Messenger brings new teachings, and it is upon these teachings that a civilization is founded. The Messengers establish new beliefs and attitudes about what is possible, and create new values and norms of behaviour which are appropriate to the times. These raise the level of religious, scientific and cultural understanding from one age to the next:

> All men have been created to carry forward an ever-advancing civilization. The Almighty beareth Me witness: To act like the beast of the field is unworthy of man. Those virtues that befit his dignity are forbearance, mercy, compassion and loving-kindness towards all the peoples and kindreds of the earth. GWB:CIX

The age in which we live is witnessing a profound change in the attitudes it holds, the values it shares, and the way it does things. The closing years of the twentieth century are turbulent times, as the process of rolling up the old world order and laying out the new one proceeds. The times are turbulent because, whereas in the past change came about slowly, the current rate of change in our world is now visible within our own lifetime. The way we appraise civilization is also changing. We are now beginning to recognize that civilization is comprised of spiritual values and ethical standards as well as of material culture and technological achievement. For civilization to be progressive and sustaining, it must be self-renewing — its institutions must incorporate the ability to adapt to the changing challenges of the times. The institutions of the Bahá'í Faith reflect this facility and they are offered to the world as a possible model for social development.

15 · THE ADMINISTRATION OF THE BAHÁ'Í FAITH

In His writings, Bahá'u'lláh forbids the creation of any form of priesthood or clergy among His followers. For this reason, there are no priests, clerics, mullahs, monks, rabbis, gurus, pastors, preachers, reverends or ministers in the Bahá'í Faith. In bygone ages, when the general population was for the most part illiterate, this kind of religious leader served a very important social rôle in the spiritual education of mankind. He was responsible for teaching the religion and representing its interests. In his capacity as teacher, the religious leader made the words of the Messenger of God accessible to people and answered questions about the Messenger's teachings.

Much historical credit must be given to these people because there were times when, if it had not been for their work, the light of religion would have gone out. In this age, however, in which the level of education has risen to the point where individuals can learn to read for themselves the Words of God, there is no longer a need for this kind of religious rôle. To perpetuate a clergy now would only be to substitute the opinions of the individual for the authority of the written word of God.

Although there are no religious leaders in the Bahá'í Faith, however, the religion is highly organized. Bahá'u'lláh

Bahá'í House of Worship, Apia, Western Samoa

established a system of administration which entrusts the authority to administer, adjudicate and legislate the affairs of the religion into the hands of elected institutions which are consultative in nature and presently composed of nine people. There are three levels of these administrative bodies: local, national and international. For example, the Local Spiritual Assembly of the Bahá'ís of Oxford is composed of nine annually elected individuals; the National Spiritual Assembly of the Bahá'ís of the United Kingdom is also elected each year; and an international convention is held every five years for the election of the Universal House of Justice. This is the supreme administrative body of the Bahá'í Faith and has the responsibility for guiding its progress and development. The Universal House of Justice has its seat at the Bahá'í World Centre on Mount Carmel, in the Holy Land.

In addition to these elected bodies, Bahá'u'lláh made provision for appointed institutions whose function is to act as learned advisers to the elected institutions. The responsibility of informing others about the Message of Bahá'u'lláh, however, rests on the shoulders of every individual Bahá'í. It is their duty to study the writings of Bahá'u'lláh for themselves, and to the best of their ability incorporate His teaching into their daily lives, so that when they are asked about the principles of the Bahá'í Faith, they can both describe and demonstrate these principles. They are, in a sense, offering themselves as an example of their faith in action, and the Bahá'í Faith is thus a religion in which one's deeds speak louder than one's words.

PART 4
THE BAHÁ'Í WAY
OF LIFE

16·THE POWER OF PRAYER AND MEDITATION

The Bahá'í Faith is both a religion and a way of life. Bahá'u'lláh does not make a distinction between the two – what people believe should be reflected in what they do. In His writings, Bahá'u'lláh repeatedly reminds His followers that the teachings of God must be manifested in one's deeds and integrated into one's life:

Let deeds, not words, be your adorning. PHW:5

There are many distinctive aspects to the Bahá'í way of life, but I shall describe only a few of them here. Among these, perhaps the most fundamental is the rôle of prayer in daily life. In one form or another, prayer is an integral part of every religion, but in this age its definition has been expanded so that it now encompasses feelings, thoughts, words and actions.

First, however, it is important to look at the purpose of prayer itself. This is not something which has always been clear and evident to me. When I was a child I used to say my bedtime prayers kneeling beside my bed with my mother watching over me. I used to say: 'Now I lay me down to sleep, I pray the Lord my soul to keep, but if I should die before

I wake, I pray the Lord my soul to take ...' This would be followed by a long list of people I should not forget in my prayers: 'Bless mommy and daddy and grandma and granddad and ...'

After saying my prayers, being tucked in and kissed goodnight, I would lie awake in the darkness and ask myself, Why should people pray? If God was All-Knowing, then He already knew what we wanted and needed without our having to ask. What was the point in praying? Did God need me to worship Him? The more I thought about this, the less I understood about prayer. Finally, I stopped thinking about it because I stopped praying. I was getting too old to be tucked in or stood over. I still believed in God but I regarded prayer as useless. By the time I found the Bahá'í Faith, I was beginning to suspect that all along I had been asking the wrong questions about prayer. Day-to-day living had taught me that some questions can be so loaded with presuppositions that people do not know where to look for the answers.

In studying the Bahá'í Faith, I began to see that it was the individual, not God, who benefited from the experience of prayer. Prayer was for our sake, not His. With regard to who needed what, I had been looking in the wrong direction — upwards instead of inwards. Now I could understand the purpose of prayer and that the impulse to pray was a natural one. People pray because they love God. The created loves the Creator. The love of God is all around us, and prayer is a means of receiving it. In the *Hidden Words*, Bahá'u'lláh explains the nature of Divine love:

> O Son of Being! Love Me, that I may love thee. If thou lovest Me not, My love can in no wise reach thee. Know this, O servant. AHW:5

Understanding the purpose of prayer was only the beginning. I started praying again, but now they were not the bed time prayers of childhood. Now I chose a moment when no one was home and read the prayers. On my thirteenth birthday, my mother gave me a Bahá'í prayer book and I had soon memorized many of them from constant use. I had my favourites:

> O God! O God! This is a broken-winged bird and his flight is very slow — assist him so that he may fly towards the apex of prosperity and salvation, wing his way with the utmost joy and happiness throughout the illimitable space, raise his melody in Thy Supreme Name in all the regions, exhilarate the ears with this call, brighten the eyes by beholding the signs of guidance.
>
> O Lord! I am single, alone and lowly. For me there is no support save Thee, no helper except Thee and sustainer beside Thee. Confirm me in Thy service, assist me with the cohorts of Thy angels, make me victorious in the promotion of Thy Word and suffer to speak out Thy wisdom amongst Thy creatures. Verily, Thou art the helper of the weak and the defender of the little ones, and verily Thou art the Powerful, the Mighty and the Unconstrained. BP:189

As I continued to study the Bahá'í writings, prayer became part of my way of life. A part of each day was reserved for prayer and reading from the Holy Scriptures of Bahá'u'lláh. It was like water to a thirsty soul. As Bahá'u'lláh has written:

> The prayerful condition is the best of all conditions, for man in such a state communeth with God, especially when prayer is offered in private and at times when one's mind is free ... Indeed, prayer imparteth life. TBV1:85

The more I prayed, the more I realized that prayer is a spiritual language which is not bounded by the limitations of the syllables and sounds of the spoken word, it is a language of the heart rather than the tongue. Prayer emanates from within in an effort to communicate with God, it is more than words, it is a spiritual attitude. The sincere feeling of love towards God in one's heart, the silent remembrance of His bounty, and the thought of thanksgiving for His mercy are all aspects of prayer. Bahá'u'lláh reveals that all the different levels on which we endeavour to communicate with God are valid, whether the prayer is found on the lips of someone praising his Creator, in the spiritual and mental attitudes we develop in the course of our lives, or in the selfless service we render others. These are all forms of prayer.

In the Bahá'í Faith, prayer is seen as a fundamental obligation for one's spiritual progress and the well-being of the world in general. To instill within us the habit of remembering God, Bahá'u'lláh has given His followers certain prayers which are to be used daily. He has provided us with three different styles, and Bahá'ís are free to select from these the one which is the most convenient and culturally familiar. The first of these prayers is to be said at any time during the day and requires about fifteen minutes to complete. The second is shorter and designed to be recited three times a day at morning, noon and evening. The third and shortest one of the three is to be recited each day around noon:

> I bear witness, O my God, that Thou hast created me to know Thee and to worship Thee. I testify, at this moment, to my powerlessness and to Thy might, to my poverty and to Thy wealth.
> There is no other God but thee the Help in Peril, the Self-Subsisting. BP:4

Each of these daily prayers reminds us of the purpose of our existence and the greatness of our Creator. Like all Bahá'í prayers, they are to be spoken aloud in the privacy of one's room:

> The reason why privacy hath been enjoined in moments of devotion is this, that thou mayest give thy best attention to the remembrance of God . . . SWB:93

Among Persian or Arabic speakers, the prayers are often chanted, while in other languages they are often set to music. In whatever form they are offered, be it spoken, chanted or sung, Bahá'í prayers soon become a vital part of one's day.

Whereas meditation is communication with one's own inner being, prayer is communication between the individual and the Creator. Prayer is the transforming power which enkindles the fire of the heart and not only benefits the spiritual progress of the individual but the world around him or her. Prayer has a positive influence on the life and soul of the individual even if at first it cannot be perceived. Although personally worded prayers are sincere and heard by God, Bahá'ís understand that there is a special power in the revealed word of God. Bahá'u'lláh has provided us with many prayers of adoration, glorification, thanksgiving, and supplication.

A Bahá'í prayer book brings together a selection of prayers which are grouped by subject. The following are just a few examples. Concerning the acquisition of spiritual qualities, Bahá'u'lláh writes:

From the sweet-scented streams of Thine eternity give me to drink, O my God, and of the fruits of the tree of Thy being enable me to taste, O my Hope! From the crystal springs of Thy love suffer me to quaff, O my Glory, and beneath the shadow of Thine everlasting providence let me abide, O my Light! Within the meadows of Thy nearness, before Thy presence, make me able to roam, O my Beloved, and at the right hand of the throne of Thy mercy, seat me, O my Desire! From the fragrant breezes of Thy joy let a breath pass over me, O my Goal, and into the heights of the paradise of Thy reality let me gain admission, O my Adored One! To the melodies of the dove of Thy oneness suffer me to harken, O Resplendent One, and through the spirit of Thy power and Thy might quicken me, O my Provider! In the spirit of Thy love keep me steadfast, O my Succourer, and in the path of Thy good pleasure set firm my steps, O my Maker! Within the garden of Thine immortality, before Thy countenance, let me abide for ever, O thou Who art merciful unto me, and upon the seat of Thy glory stablish me, O Thou Who art my Possessor! To the heaven of Thy loving-kindness lift me up, O my Quickener, and unto the Daystar of Thy guidance lead me, O Thou my Attractor! Before the revelations of Thine invisible spirit summon me to be present, O Thou Who art my Origin and my Highest Wish, and unto the essence of the fragrance of Thy beauty, which Thou wilt manifest, cause me to return, O Thou Who art my God!

Potent art Thou to do what pleaseth Thee. Thou art, verily, the Most Exalted, the All-Glorious, the All-Highest.

Regarding healing:

Thy name is my healing, O my God, and remembrance of Thee is my remedy. Nearness to Thee is my hope, and love for Thee is my companion. Thy mercy to me is my healing and my succour in both this world and the world to come. Thou, verily, art the All-Bountiful, the All-Knowing, the All-Wise. PB:87

For the establishment of unity:

O my God! O my God! Unite the hearts of Thy servants and reveal to them Thy great purpose. May they follow Thy commandments and abide in Thy law. Help them, O God, in their endeavour, and grant them strength to serve Thee. O God! Leave them not to themselves, but guide their steps by the light of Thy knowledge, and cheer their hearts by Thy love. Verily, Thou art their Helper and their Lord. PB:204

In praise and gratitude of God:

All praise, O my God, be to Thee Who art the Source of all glory and majesty, of greatness and honour, of sovereignty and dominion, of loftiness and grace, of awe and power. Whomsoever Thou willest Thou causest to draw nigh unto the Most Great Ocean, and on whomsoever Thou desirest Thou conferrest the honour of recognizing Thy Most Ancient Name. Of all who are in heaven and on earth, none can withstand the operation of Thy sovereign Will. From all eternity Thou didst rule the entire creation, and Thou wilt continue for evermore to exercise Thy dominion over all created things. There is none other God but Thee, the Almighty, the Most Exalted, the All-powerful, the All-Wise.

Illumine, O Lord, the faces of Thy servants, that they may behold Thee; and cleanse their hearts that they may turn unto the court of Thy heavenly favours, and recognize Him Who is the Manifestation of Thy Self and the Dayspring of Thine Essence. Verily, Thou art the Lord of all worlds. There is no God but thee, the Unconstrained, the All-Subduing. BP:120

As can be perceived from the content of the above selection from the writings of Bahá'u'lláh, prayer is about the acquisition of spiritual qualities and attuning our wants with what God desires for us. Prayer should not merely be a wish-list of things like a child's letter to Santa Claus:

The true worshipper, while praying, should endeavour not so much to ask God to fulfil his wishes and desires, but rather to adjust these and make them conform to the Divine Will. Only through such an attitude can one derive that feeling of inner peace and contentment which the power of prayer alone can confer. CIB:26/10/38

These prayers impart a mental attitude which is conducive to spiritual growth, but like everything else in the Bahá'í way of life, moderation is important if the individual is going to get anything out of the experience:

Should a person recite but a single verse from the Holy Writings in a spirit of joy and radiance, this would be better for him than reciting wearily all the Scriptures of God . . .

Prayer is part of the practical process of spiritual guidance which extends beyond worship. It is a process which assists decision-making, and helps in the selection of appropriate actions. Although there are no dogmas or precise formulas within the Bahá'í Faith, there are at least five practical stages in the process of prayer and meditation:

1. Prayer
2. Meditation
3. Inspiration
4. Volition and Faith
5. Action

The process always begins with prayer. The individual who seeks enlightenment will use prayer as a means of turning his or her heart towards God as the Source of all knowledge. As Bahá'u'lláh has written:

> Intone, O My servant, the verses of God that have been received by thee, as intoned by them who have drawn nigh unto Him, that the sweetness of thy melody may kindle thine own soul, and attract the hearts of all men. Whoso reciteth, in the privacy of his own chamber, the verses revealed by God, the scattering angels of the Almighty shall scatter abroad the fragrance of the words uttered by his mouth, and shall cause the heart of every righteous man to throb. Though he may, at first, remain unaware of its effect, yet the virtue of the grace vouchsafed unto him must needs sooner or later exercise its influence upon his soul. Thus have the mysteries of the Revelation of God been decreed by virtue of the Will of Him Who is the Source of power and wisdom.

Prayer is then followed by meditation. Meditation is not the emptying the mind of all thought. It is the focusing of the mind on to a subject without external distractions. It is an art

Bahá'í House of Worship, Panama City, Panama

which takes practice to perfect. The more people use meditation, the more they discover its power to restore a sense of tranquillity and purpose. It is during this meditative period that people wait for the inspiration which will come.

Inspiration comes both from within and without. As many artists have tried to describe, inspiration is received rather than found. In one place in the Bahá'í writings, inspiration is explained as follows:

> This faculty brings forth from the invisible plane the science and arts. Through the meditative faculty inventions are made possible, colossal undertakings are carried out; through it governments can run smoothly. Through this faculty man enters into the very Kingdom of God ... Through the faculty of meditation man attains to eternal life; through it he receives the breath of the Holy Spirit ... Meditation is the key for opening the doors of mysteries. In that state man abstracts himself; in that state man withdraws himself from all outside objects; in that subjective mood he is immersed in the ocean of spiritual life and can unfold the secrets of things-in-themselves ... It is an axiomatic fact that while you meditate you are speaking with your own spirit. In that state of mind you put certain questions to your spirit and the spirit answers; the light breaks forth and the reality is revealed ... The meditative faculty is akin to the mirror: if you put it before earthly objects it will reflect them. Therefore, if the spirit of man is contemplating earthly objects he will be informed of these. But if you turn the mirror of your spirits heavenwards, the heavenly constellations and the Sun of Reality will be reflected in your hearts, and the virtues of the Kingdom will be obtained ... May we indeed become mirrors reflecting the heavenly realities, and may we become so pure as to reflect the stars of heaven. PT:174

Volition is essential to the next stage. Volition is the will-power to put into action the ideas and inspiration which have been received. Personal volition is vital if the individual is to be successful. Faith is also required. The individual must acquire an attitude of mind which believes that the inspiration is possible. Faith here is akin to visualization. The individual should be able to see the idea implemented and behave as if it has already been achieved.

Finally, action. The purpose and product of the prayer and meditative process is the practical application of the inspiration the individual has received. This process is a problem-solving mechanism for the individual, and the source and avenue of inspiration to the artist and scientist, the writer and professional person:

Prayer and meditation are very important in deepening the spiritual life of the individual, but with them must go also action and example, as these are the tangible results of the former. Both are essential. CIB:15/06/44

It is not sufficient to pray diligently for guidance, but this prayer must be followed by meditation as to the best methods of action and then action itself.

17·CONSULTATION AND UNIVERSAL PARTICIPATION

Consultation and universal participation are fundamental and distinctive aspects of the Bahá'í way of life. They are the means of collective problem-solving and decision-making within the Bahá'í community. Consultation and universal participation are seen to be as inseparable as bricks and mortar, and together they support the edifice of the Bahá'í administrative institutions. Consultation and universal participation are part of the practical philosophy of the religion, and the union of these two concepts allows the Bahá'í Faith to progress and develop. Philosophically, they supersede the need for any form of clergy.

Take ye counsel together in all matters, inasmuch as consultation is the lamp of guidance which leadeth the way, and is the bestower of understanding.

Bahá'í consultation is more than a religious council or conference called to consider a particular matter. It is an integral part of the formal and informal decision-making process among all Bahá'ís. It is defined by the full and frank participation of the entire community in which every individual has the right and responsibility to have and offer his or her opinion. Bahá'í consultation is democratic in nature. I know that democracy means different things to different people, but the process of consultation and the expectation of universal participation within the Bahá'í Faith allows people openly to discuss matters of common concern and ultimately to reach decisions by voting as individuals for ideas. Bahá'ís vote on the merit of the idea and not the personality of the one who proposes it. In this sense, Bahá'í consultation employs a very unpolitical form of democracy. The process tends to unite the participants rather than divide them, and in so doing Bahá'í consultation offers a real alternative to traditional political thinking. It replaces the mentality which sees as appropriate such devices as bilateral debate, personality attacks, flattery, manipulation, coercion, collusion, the exchange of political assistance, lobbying, or the development of special-interest groups, parties, or factions. In the Bahá'í Faith, these are seen as elements of an old world order, and ethically bankrupt.

There is no specific step-by-step guide to the process of Bahá'í consultation, but the following sequence will give the reader a fairly clear picture of the process:

1. Spiritual and emotional preparation;
2. Establishment of mutual trust;
3. Frank and non-aggressive participation;
4. Collective consideration of ideas;
5. Non-personalization of ideas;
6. Problem definition;
7. Gathering possible solutions;
8. Refinement of solution;
9. The process of reaching a consensus;
10. Humble submission to the will of the majority;
11. Collective and affirmative action.

The process of Bahá'í consultation requires both spiritual and emotional preparation. Before the community meets the individuals pray and meditate as described above to prepare themselves spiritually for consultation. This assures that they are spiritually and emotionally refreshed, and prepared to contribute to the decision-making process. This preparation is important:

> True consultation is spiritual conference in the attitude and atmosphere of love.

The process is dependent upon the establishment of a mutual trust based upon courtesy, respect and the good behaviour of the participants. This is important because if consultation is to be beneficial, participation must be universal; mutual trust assures universal participation. This is true whether there are two or twenty people involved. Mutual trust is essential because this kind of participation does not mean merely waiting for an opportunity to speak. When one person speaks, all the rest carefully attend, sincerely trying to understand the point of view of the speaker. During the consultative process, listening constitutes about ninety per cent of one's participation. Once the participants have experienced this process several times with the same people, a profound mutual trust and respect develop. This trust empowers people to solve the kind of problems which require co-operation.

The Bahá'í consultative process is one of truth-seeking, not opinion-forcing. Everyone's opinion is regarded as equally valid, and as truth is relative to the sum total of collective understanding, the only way to discover what action would be appropriate is to have the frank participation of everyone involved. Each participant offers his or her opinion as an approximation and not an absolute, with the humble understanding that the total result will be greater than the sum of the individual contributions. Bahá'í consultation is both frank and loving; it is held in a non-aggressive atmosphere in which all the participants tacitly acknowledge from the outset the willingness to change their mind if a better idea emerges. In this way, opinions will clash but not individuals:

> The shining spark of truth cometh only after the clash of differing opinions.

The ideas which do emerge are considered collectively on their own merit and do not reflect on the personalities of the participants. The egos of the individuals are eclipsed by the ideas themselves. With this in mind, participants will know that the ideas they propose will be heard and considered fairly without having to be repeated or insisted upon:

> They must in every matter search out the truth and not insist upon their own opinion, for stubbornness and persistence in one's views will lead ultimately to discord and wrangling and the truth will remain hidden.

For this to be achieved, the participants must adopt a new philosophical attitude which allows for the non-personalization of ideas. This means simply that during the consultative process, their individual ideas are not their personal property. When a participant gives his or her opinion or proposes a solution, it is offered to the entire group. Once it is said, it is no longer the individual's point of view, but rather one of the ideas which has emerged from the consultation. In a sense, all ideas belong to the entire group. There is great benefit in adopting this attitude. If the idea is adopted, modified, amended or rejected then the individual who suggested it feels no personal triumph or defeat. This helps to remove the possibility of politics within the Bahá'í consultative process – without egos, politics dies from neglect.

Defining the problem is crucial to finding a solution, and only by listening to the perceptions of others can a collective problem be described and assessed. People see the world differently and there is great value in having access to a different perspective. Bahá'í consultation provides that access. If people are unaccustomed or unable to listen with empathy to the insights of others, then they are doomed to living in a world where their social perspective is exclusively personal. The habit of personalizing everything is a seriously incapacitating form of social blindness. Bahá'ís try to get away from the habit of relating to any problem with the words 'What about me?' Collective insight is the key to solving collective problems.

The great advantage of this type of consultation is that it allows people to consider several possible solutions to a particular problem. It is only when several plausible ideas are laid side by side and compared, not for their absolute rightness or wrongness but for their relative appropriateness, that there emerges a spectrum of possible solutions.

There is a propensity in Western civilization to think in terms of monocausalism and monosolutionalism. Many people tend to think along the lines of THE problem and THE solution. (I concede that this is a sweeping generalization, and that there are many other groups which do not think along these lines, but the propensity is still there among a considerable portion of the population.) Bahá'í consultation overcomes this monocausal and monosolutional mentality. And by attaching the word *Bahá'í* to this type of consultation, I am not implying that Bahá'ís hold some kind of philosophical patent or copyright on the concepts they employ. Ideas are born, but they then belong to all of mankind. The adjective *Bahá'í* is descriptive, not possessive.

Once all the participants have offered their ideas, and a selection of possible solutions has emerged from the consultation, the process of refinement begins. Many of the suggestions will be similar and their good points can be amalgamated. Eventually by weighing the merits of each possible solution, the most appropriate ones will be voted upon by the group.

Voting is the process by which the group reaches a consensus. Each participant has an equal vote, and either endorses or rejects the proposed solution. Within the Bahá'í consultative process there are no abstentions – universal participation is required at all stages of the process. Certainly, selecting a solution by unanimous consensus would be ideal, but if this is not possible, then the majority will decide whether the proposal should be adopted or not.

Next comes what is probably the most important part of the process. All the individual participants must lend their unstinting and earnest support to the decision of the majority. This kind of humble and sincere submission to the will of consensus is often the hardest thing to learn within the Bahá'í consultative process. The concept of proponents and opponents is so deeply ingrained in the mentality of modern-day social rôle-models like governmental and corporate organizations, that people initially doubt there is any other way. It seems natural for people to withdraw their support and wait on the sidelines for their chance to say 'I told you so', if their idea has not been accepted, and when failure comes, to feel vindicated.

This is a very destructive attitude. The act of withholding support by a minority never allows people to realize the full potential of a good idea, or the true worthlessness of a bad one. This underlying opposition and lack of unity very often leads to the desolation of the entire group. There is, however, great wisdom in wholeheartedly supporting the decision of the majority. Not only can any hidden potential be readily seen, but it is also the quickest way of determining whether the solution the group has chosen is correct or not.

Submission to the will of the majority is part of the mutual trust which develops within Bahá'í consultation. Participants soon understand that not all decisions are correct, even the ones reached by unanimous consensus. If something is going to go wrong, universal participation will very quickly reveal it. A great deal of time is saved which would otherwise be wasted trying to do something halfheartedly. Once they have tried this type of consultation, those who initially doubted that a concept such as submission to the will of the majority could be beneficial to the assessment of collective decision-making, soon become its greatest champions and find it hard to believe that others have not yet discovered its worth. It truly empowers people to achieve success:

No power can exist except through unity. No welfare and no well-being can be attained except through consultation.

We now come to the final stage – the goal of the Bahá'í consultative process. While most people have at some time found themselves in a meeting which seemed to exist for the sole purpose of planning other meetings, the process of Bahá'í consultation avoids this altogether. The discussion and decision-making process must be followed by collective and affirmative *action*. The solutions must be implemented, as I have stated, with the support of all the participants. This is the reason why consultation exists – words must become actions.

Bahá'í House of Worship, New Delhi, India

18·SERVICE TO HUMANITY

The brief span of time we have here on earth is our most precious possession. Life is a wondrous time of discovery, progress and fulfilment. Life, however, is not just a personal experience; it is shared with the rest of humanity. Our time here is not merely an individualistic preparation for the next stage in our personal spiritual development, but a priceless opportunity to assist in the social development of the planet. It is our personal and collective responsibility to leave this planet in a better condition than that in which we found it.

There are so many problems to solve in the world today – poverty, disease, ignorance, hatred and oppression – that it requires the concerted effort of everyone to overcome them and replace them with abundance, health, education, love and unity. Bahá'ís work to achieve these goals. Both of the distinctive aspects of the Bahá'í way of life described above reflect this: as individuals, Bahá'ís pray and meditate on how best to serve mankind; and collectively they consult together towards this same end.

> Blessed and happy is he that ariseth to promote the best interests of the peoples and kindreds of the earth.
> TB:167

Service to mankind is an integral part of being a Bahá'í. It is reflected in the Bahá'í attitude towards concepts such as work, motives, and achievement: work done in the spirit of service is a form of worship; the purity of one's motives is more important than the result of one's actions; and in achievements, the process is just as important as the product. It is a philosophy of deeds which replaces the anarchic belief that the ends justify the means. In the Bahá'í Faith, the means *are* the ends.

Fundamental to the concept of service is the belief that personal morality and ethical social behaviour are of great benefit to the progress of mankind. No one is powerless to effect beneficial change. Each person should see themselves as a significant component of the world; we should never feel helpless or insignificant. Everyone has the ability to help the world on many different levels. We can be productive individuals, responsible consumers, loving husbands and wives, exemplary parents, honourable sons and daughters, considerate neighbours, and good citizens, all at the same time. Basically, we all have the responsibility to be environmentally friendly to the spiritual, social, emotional and physical well-being of the planet. All these elements of service help the condition of the world immensely.

Beyond one's personal morality and ethical social behaviour, everyone is endowed with skills and talents which are useful to mankind on a professional level. Personal capacity is often dependent upon health and opportunity, but fulfilling one's capacity is everyone's duty. The person who has employed all of his few talents to the betterment of the planet is of greater value to mankind than the person who has a multiplicity of talents but selfishly uses them solely for his own benefit:

> O son of man! If thine eyes be turned towards mercy, forsake the things that profit thee and cleave unto that which will profit mankind. And if thine eyes be turned towards justice, choose thou for thy neighbour that which thou choosest for thyself. Humility exalteth man to the heaven of glory and power, whilst pride

abaseth him to the depths of wretchedness and degradation. TB:64

The concept of service extends beyond the Bahá'ís themselves. The Bahá'í Faith as a religion supports the non-governmental activities of the United Nations and the European Community in their efforts to overcome the political differences which divide us, and organizations like the Worldwide Fund for Nature which work toward understanding the planet's ecology and improving the environment. Bahá'u'lláh exhorted His followers to serve mankind in whatever way they could:

Address yourselves to the promotion of the well-being and tranquillity of the children of men. Bend your minds and wills to the education of the peoples and kindreds of the earth, that haply the dissensions that divide it may, through the power of the Most Great Name, be blotted out from its face, and all mankind become the upholders of one Order, and the inhabitants of one City. GWB:CLVI

Ultimately, everyone who becomes a Bahá'í brings his or her talents and experience to the religion, and contributes to the range of services the Bahá'í Faith can offer the world.

19·THE BAHÁ'Í EXPERIENCE

Being a Bahá'í and part of the community is a very distinctive way of life. In addition to its basic teachings, the Bahá'í Faith also has its own Festivals, Holy Days and calendar. The Bahá'í year begins on 21st March, with the celebration of Naw-Rúz, the Bahá'í New Year. This is the first day of spring, the equinox.

There are nineteen months in the Bahá'í calendar, and each month contains nineteen days. This gives a total of 361 days. There are four additional intercalary days, or days between the months, during normal years and five during leap years, to complete the requisite number of annual days.

Each Bahá'í month is named in Arabic after an attribute of God. Either numbers or names denote the day of the month. If the name is used then the names of the days of the month follow the same sequence as the names of the months. For example, in the Bahá'í calendar the 4th of July 1963, the date I became a Bahá'í, is:

11 Rahmat 121 BE, or the day of Mashíyyat of the month Rahmat in the 121st year of the Bahá'í Era

The Bahá'í Era began with the Declaration of the Báb on the 23rd of May 1844 and will end at some future date with the appearance of the next Messenger of God. Bahá'u'lláh promised that the Bahá'í Era would last not less than a thousand years.

At the beginning of every Bahá'í month, the Bahá'ís gather and celebrate the Nineteen Day Feast. The following is a list of the first day of each Bahá'í month:

21 March	Bahá	Splendour
9 April	Jalál	Glory
28 April	Jamál	Beauty
17 May	'Azamat	Grandeur
5 June	Núr	Light
24 June	Rahmat	Mercy
13 July	Kalimát	Words
1 August	Kamál	Perfection
20 August	Asmá'	Names
8 September	'Izzat	Might
27 September	Mashíyyat	Will
16 October	'Ilm	Knowledge
4 November	Qudrat	Power
23 November	Qawl	Speech
12 December	Masá'il	Questions
31 December	Sharaf	Honour
19 January	Sultán	Sovereignty
7 February	Mulk	Dominion
2 March	'Alá'	Loftiness

The Nineteen Day Feast brings together members of the Bahá'í community for worship, consultation and fellowship. It is an occasion of hospitality and unity. The programme for each Nineteen Day Feast is divided into three parts to correspond to these purposes. The devotional portion consists of reading primarily from the writings of Bahá'u'lláh, the Báb and 'Abdu'l-Bahá, and occasionally from the sacred scriptures of other religions; the purpose of the consultative portion is to enable individual Bahá'ís to offer suggestions to the Local Spiritual Assembly of the town or city; and the social portion consists of serving refreshments and offering fellowship.

There is no set service. Whoever has offered to host the

Nineteen Day Feast is free to select which writings are read, and sometimes there may be music or singing, depending on the musical talents of the Bahá'ís in the community. The refreshments are either supplied by the host or contributed by the Bahá'ís who attend. The form the Nineteen Day Feast takes is not as important as the spirit it generates. As Bahá'u'lláh has written:

> It hath been enjoined upon you once a month to offer hospitality, even should ye serve no more than water; for God hath willed to bind your hearts together, though it be through heavenly and earthly means combined. NDF:1

During the year there are certain Bahá'í Holy Days on which work is suspended:

21 March	Naw-Rúz, the Bahá'í New Year
21 April	The First Day of Ridván
29 April	The Ninth Day of Ridván
2 May	The Twelfth Day of Ridván
23 May	The Declaration of the Báb
29 May	The Ascension of Bahá'u'lláh
9 July	The Martyrdom of the Báb
20 October	The Birth of the Báb
12 November	The Birth of Bahá'u'lláh

Two further days associated with the life of 'Abdu'l-Bahá, the son of Bahá'u'lláh, are also commemorated but on these days work is not prohibited:

26 November	The Day of the Covenant
28 November	The Ascension of 'Abdu'l-Bahá

The Intercalary Days, or Ayyám-i-Há, occur between the 26th of February and the 1st of March inclusive. These are set aside as days of preparation for the Fast – days of hospitality, charity and the giving of gifts. Bahá'u'lláh has given us the following prayer for these days:

My God, my Fire and my Light! The days which Thou hast named Ayyám-i-Há in Thy Book have begun, O Thou Who art the King of names, and the fast which Thy most exalted Pen hath enjoined unto all who are in the kingdom of Thy creation to observe is approaching. I entreat Thee, O my Lord, by these days and by all such as have during that period clung to the cord of Thy commandments, and laid hold on the handle of Thy precepts, to grant that unto every soul may be assigned a place within the precincts of Thy court, and a seat at the revelation of the splendours of the light of Thy countenance. PMB:49

The fasting period within the Bahá'í Faith lasts nineteen days, one Bahá'í month. The month of 'Alá' (Loftiness) is the last month of the Bahá'í year. It is a period of abstinence from food and drink, from sunrise to sunset. For those Bahá'ís who smoke, the Fast also applies to smoking during the same daylight hours. Bahá'u'lláh has granted exemption for those younger than fifteen and older than seventy, and for those who are ill or travelling. Exemption is further granted to women who are pregnant, breast-feeding or menstruating. The purpose of the Fast is renewal:

It is essentially a period of meditation and prayer, of spiritual recuperation, during which the believer must strive to make the necessary readjustments in his inner life, and to refresh and reinvigorate the spiritual forces latent in his soul. Its significance and purpose are, therefore, fundamentally spiritual in character. Fasting is symbolic, and a reminder of abstinence from selfish and carnal desires. LG:487

The fasting ends with Naw-Rúz Festival, the Bahá'í New Year. This is a joyous time in which the Bahá'í community gathers and celebrates not only the end of the Fast but the beginning of a new year. 'Abdu'l-Bahá, the son of Bahá'u'lláh, described Naw-Rúz in the following words:

This sacred day, when the sun illumines equally the whole earth, is called the equinox, and the equinox is the symbol of the Manifestation of God. The Sun of Truth rises on the horizon of Divine Mercy and sends forth its rays. This day is consecrated to commemorate it. It is the beginning of Spring. When the sun appears at the equinox, it causes a movement in all living things. The mineral world is set in motion, plants begin to shoot, the desert is changed into a prairie, trees bud and every living thing responds, including the bodies of animal and men.

The rising of the sun at the equinox is the symbol of life, and likewise it is the symbol of the Divine Manifestation of God, for the rising of the Sun of Truth in the heaven of Divine Bounty established the signal of life for the world. The human reality begins to live, our thoughts are transformed and our intelligence is quickened. The Sun of Truth bestows Eternal Life, just as the solar sun is the cause of terrestrial life. SWV5N1:4

In addition to these Nineteen Day Feasts and Holy Day observances, Bahá'ís organize other meetings throughout the year to which they invite friends who are interested in knowing more about Bahá'u'lláh and His teachings. These meetings – sometimes called 'Firesides' – are very informal and are held either in the homes of individual Bahá'ís or at a Bahá'í Centre. Personally, I do not know the origin of the expression Fireside, but it dates back at least to the beginning of this century. At a Fireside, people are free to ask any questions they wish about the Bahá'í Faith, and during the course of an evening, the conversation usually ranges far and wide. Discussions will often centre around a particular theme such as unity, women's rights, the environment, world peace, the rainforests, or life after death.

Being a Bahá'í is about belonging to an international community of people from diverse racial, cultural and religious heritages who are working together to bring about world peace.

Wherever people reside there is usually a well-established Bahá'í community nearby. Becoming a Bahá'í is a personal decision and experience. There are no initiation ceremonies in the Bahá'í Faith – in fact there are no ceremonies at all. Quite simply, the Bahá'ís are the people who recognize Bahá'u'lláh as the Messenger of God for this age. People will know from reading the writings of Bahá'u'lláh whether they are Bahá'ís. Informing the National Bahá'í Centre of their decision puts new Bahá'ís in contact with other Bahá'ís.

If you feel you would like to register as a Bahá'í or obtain more information on the Bahá'í Faith, look in the telephone book for the Bahá'í Community nearest you or write to one of the addresses at the back of this book. I have included only a few of the hundreds of addresses possible. If you live outside these countries, any of the Bahá'í Centres listed can put you into contact with Bahá'ís in your own country.

I do not know of any appropriate way to end a book about the Bahá'í Faith. There is a lifetime of wonder and inspiration to be derived from the Bahá'í writings, and it is my whole-hearted hope that you will take the time to investigate more fully the teachings of Bahá'u'lláh and decide for yourself whether the Bahá'í Faith is for you. Perhaps it is befitting to leave you with Bahá'u'lláh's own words:

Strive, O people, that your eyes may be directed towards the mercy of God, that your hearts may be attuned to His wondrous remembrance, that your souls may rest confidently upon His grace and bounty, that your feet may tread the path of His good-pleasure. GWB:296

BIBLIOGRAPHY

Abdu'l-Bahá, *The Promulgation of Universal Peace: Talks Delivered by 'Abdu'l-Bahá during His Visit to the United States and Canada in 1912*, comp. H MacNutt, 2nd ed. (Wilmette, Il: Bahá'í Publishing Trust, 1982).

Abdu'l-Bahá, *Paris Talks: Addresses Given by 'Abdu'l-Bahá in Paris in 1911–1912*, 11th ed. (London: Bahá'í Publishing Trust, 1971).

Bahá'u'lláh, *Tablets of Bahá'u'lláh Revealed after the Kitáb-i-Aqdas*, comp. Research Department of the Universal House of Justice, trans. Habib Taherzadeh and others, rev. ed. (Haifa: Bahá'í World Centre, 1982).

Bahá'u'lláh, *Gleanings of the Writings of Bahá'u'lláh*, comp. and trans. Shoghi Effendi, 2nd rev. ed. (Wilmette, Il: Bahá'í Publishing Trust, 1976).

Bahá'u'lláh *Selections from the Writings of Bahá'u'lláh*, (Wilmette, Il: Bahá'í Publishing Committee, 1943).

Bahá'u'lláh, *Proclamation of Bahá'u'lláh to the Kings and Leaders of the World*, (Haifa: Bahá'í World Centre, 1978).

Bahá'u'lláh, *Prayers and Meditations of Bahá'u'lláh*, comp. and trans. Shoghi Effendi, rev. ed. (London: Bahá'í Publishing Trust, 1978).

Bahá'u'lláh, *The Hidden Words*, trans. Shoghi Effendi, 'with the assistance of some English friends' (London: Nightingale Books, 1992).

Bahá'u'lláh, *Epistle to the Son of the Wolf*, trans. Shoghi Effendi (Wilmette, Il: Bahá'í Publishing Trust, 1969).

Bahá'u'lláh, Báb, 'Abdu'l-Bahá, *Bahá'í Prayers* (Wilmette, Il: Bahá'í Publishing Trust, 1985).

Shoghi Effendi, *Principles of Bahá'í Administration*, 4th ed. (London: Bahá'í Publishing Trust, 1976).

Shoghi Effendi, *God Passes By*, (Wilmette, Il: Bahá'í Publishing Trust, 1970).

Star of the West, V. 1 no. 1 (Mar. 21, 1910) – V. 25 no. 12 (Mar. 1924) reprinted in eight bound volumes (Oxford: George Ronald, 1978).

Universal House of Justice, *Synopsis and codification of the Laws and Ordinances of the Kitab-í-Aqdas*, comp. Research Department of the Universal House of Justice, trans. Shoghi Effendi (Haifa: Bahá'í World Centre, 1973).

Universal House of Justice, *Lights of Guidance: A Bahá'í Reference File*, comp. Helen Hornby (New Delhi: Bahá'í Publishing Trust, 1983).

Universal House of Justice, *Nineteen Day Feast*, comp. Research Department of the Universal House of Justice (London: Bahá'í Publishing Trust, 1989).

Ann Vickers, *Prayer and Meditation*, (Southam: Spiritual Assembly of the Bahá'ís of Warwick, 1990).

ABBREVIATED TITLES USED FOR QUOTED MATERIAL

PHW: Persian Hidden Words
AHW: Arabic Hidden Words
BP: Bahá'í Prayers
SWB: Selections from the Writings of Bahá'u'lláh
CIB: Correspondence to an Individual Believer
KA: Kitab-i-Aqdas
PT: Paris Talks
PMP: Prayer and Meditation pamphlet
PBA: Principles of Bahá'í Administration
PUP: The Promulgation of Universal Peace
TB: Tablets of Bahá'u'lláh
GWB: Gleanings of the Writings of Bahá'u'lláh
NDF: Nineteen Day Feast
PMB: Prayers and Meditations of Bahá'u'lláh

LG: Lights of Guidance
SW: Star of the West
PB: Proclamation of Bahá'u'lláh
GPB: God Passes By
ESW: Epistle to the Son of the Wolf

Useful Addresses

National Bahá'í Centre
27 Rutland Gate
London SW7 1PD
United Kingdom

National Bahá'í Centre
536 Sheridan Road
Wilmette
Illinois 60091
United States of America

National Bahá'í Centre
7200 Leslie Street
Thornhill
Ontario L3T 6L8
Canada

National Bahá'í Centre
Post Box 19
New Delhi 110 001
India

National Bahá'í Centre
Post Office Box 21–551
Henderson
Auckland 8
New Zealand

National Bahá'í Centre
Post Office Box 285
Mona Vale
NSW 2103
Australia

INDEX